ECONOMICS
OF
DRAMATIC THEATRES

Economics of Dramatic Theatres

The Impact of Technologically Mediated Drama on Theatrical Performances

K.V. Joseph

SHIPRA

ISBN: 978-81-7541-879-0

First Published in India in 2016

Economics of Dramatic Theatres: The Impact of Technologically Mediated Drama on Theatrical Performances

Published by:
SHIPRA PUBLICATIONS
LG 18-19, Pankaj Central Market,
I.P. Ext., Patparganj, Delhi-110092, India
Tel.: +91 11 2223 5152/6152
E-mail: info@shiprapublication.com
www.shiprapublication.com

Preface

It is widely held that art and culture are outside the ambit of economics. The reason is that art and culture are supposed to be creative in nature with heavy dependence on intellectual rather than on material means for their productive activities. Nevertheless, both the activities require material means which can be used for alternative purposes. Naturally, economic parameters also become relevant for understanding cultural and artistic activities. At the same time, artists like other workers may demand large amount of monetary remuneration, for leading a comfortable living. Furthermore, consumers spend a portion of their scarce income for purchasing, or utilising artistic products. Naturally the calculus of consumer choice in the spending pattern of money for works of arts comes to the fore. Apparently, artistic activities fall within the purview of economics.

Drama, one of the most important cultural activities, requires fairly large quantities of both economic and cultural inputs for its very performance. Naturally it becomes a Janus- faced cultural activity with material and cultural inputs coalescing with each other. In turn, fairly high cost of production enters in the picture as a concomitant variable in any dramatic performance. How to recoup the cost naturally poses as a live issue. Dependence on the audience or some patron was the usual way out to cover the cost. As a matter of fact, some sort of a commercial dimension was discernible in dramatic performance from the very beginning of dramatic art.

With the spectacular progress in technology, some sort of a mutation has taken place in the very production and exhibition of dramatic products. Actually, what transpired was the introduction of technologically mediated drama like film and tele-serial, which according to some authors, form the seventh art. Since such dramas could be produced on factory lines with the aid of technology at very little variable cost, they could easily erode the pulling power of theatrical drama. In fact, dramatic theatres face stiff competition from the technologically mediated drama and the very survival of dramatic theatres itself is in jeopardy. Since drama is one of the important forms of art from the ancient past, the nature and gravity of the threat to drama appear as major issues requiring serious attention. The present study is a modest attempt to uncover the issues by drawing empirical evidences from Malayalam dramatic theatres.

The main thrust of the study is on the economic imperatives of drama, though it is a cultural activity. The economic imperatives were at work even during the formative stages of drama in Greece, where it was, by and large, the rich citizens, aided by their slave labour, who provided the material means. It was again the rich citizens who provided the material means to drama during the Imperial Roman period. The Church, the kings and the nobles were in the fray for rendering material support to drama throughout the Middle Ages. Once modern era ushered in, the mantle fell on the audience with the market serving as the channel for the flow of finances. Since drama is addressed to the the audience, it was easy to shift the financial burden on the audience. With market in the helm, organisational arrangements in the form of theatres or banners assumed the role in the very performance of drama.

Drama became vulnerable once mediated dramatic forms like motion pictures and television appeared in the scene, precisely because of the economic imperatives. Most of the audience and the talented actors abandoned drama mainly because of the weight of the economic compulsion. Drama, however, manages to survive, thanks to its artistic crediantials. What is lost to theatrical drama is the commercial mask that drama was wearing, once market became not merely the facilitator but also the arbiter in rendering financial leverage to drama. Nevertheless, it has lost its commanding position as a buoyant art. What is needed for its sustenance as a viable cultural activity is some sort of public support, not to be renderd to any Tom, Dick, and Harry, but to the genuine works of art. At the same time, drama on its part should think in terms of adopting new formats differing from the current proscenium model.

The study has attemptd to introduce some kind of modifications to certain concepts. The term technologically mediated drama was introduced in the study as a working definition to denote motion pictures and tele-serials etc. The intercession of technology at every stage of their production stands as the raison d'etre for such a stance. The exponents of mediated drama look upon the audience as mere consumers of a commodity. On the other hand, one of the attempts of the study is to look at them as a distinct category of people who appreciates drama rather than seeking units in "utils" of satisfaction from watching a film like a consumer. It is believed that the attempt of the author is, by and large, justifiable in this regard.

Such a study cannot be undertaken without material and financial support. In this connection, the author has been lucky to get the timely support from many sources. The Ministry of Culture, Government of India, Indian Council of Social Science Research and Kerala Council of Hitorical Research stand as the foremost agenies in rendering a helpful hand to the author in the matter. The author records his deep sense of gratitude and indebtedness to all of them.

Timely help has come from many persons connected with dramatic world for pursuing the study. Prominent among them are Dr. Vaman Kendre, the Director School of Drama, New Delhi, and Devendra Raj Ankur, a previous Director, and Dr. Shibu Kottaram, the Director, School of Drama, Trichur. The author was lucky to meet Kavalam Narayana Panicker, Dr. P.V. Krishnan Nair, and a host of persons connected with dramatic work, and to get valuable information from them. Rev. Dr. Ninan Tharakan, a former Principal and a gifted author was kind enough to go through the draft and make valuable corrections. An artist by profession, Mr. Shibu Lal has helped the author to collect the much-needed data by making a field study. The author places on record his deep sense of gratitude to all of them.

The volume would not have come to a final stage but for the facilities afforded to the author by the authorities of the KCHR, and in particular by Dr. P.J. Cherian, Director of the KCHR, Ms. Preeta Nayar, the Research Officer and the other members of the staff of the KCHR. The author expresses his thanks for the help and coordialty extended to him for the study.

Dr. K.V. Joseph

Contents

List of Tables

1

Introduction

Drama is one of the oldest forms of art with a history of more than two-thousand years. It is a combination of performing art with literary form of expression. Acting, superimposed by literary narrative, supplemented by music and dance, form the main components of drama. All these artistic performances are enacted on a stage, which needs to be decorated and adjusted to the requirements of particular dramatic scenes. Drama is performed in front of an audience. Thus a triangular relationship between artists, literary narrative and the audience is inherent in a drama.

Artistic activities rely more on mental faculties rather than on material means. However, material means are also required to meet the subsistence needs of artists. Furthermore, a cultural activity like drama has to rely more on material means, in comparison with other forms of art, since a host of artists and instruments are required for its presentation in a theatre. Ipso facto, drama becomes both an economic as well as an artistic activity since it makes use of different inputs. In turn, cost element enters in the picture in a big way in the enactment of a drama. The need for recoupment of the cost becomes inevitable in such a situation. Partly as a result of the cost element, or what can be termed economic compulsion, in the good old days of Greek drama, it was performed as a public function, in which all the citizens attended. In India, it was performed as a ritual function, enacted during religious festivals in the temples in the foregone days. Thus material support was extended by the public authorities or religious bodies in the past. However, during recent years, market has emerged as the channel for the flow of material support to drama, as in the case of many other artistic and cultural activities. Drama on its part, ensures material support by selling the ticket in the market or charging an entry fee from the audience for seeing the dramatic performance.

The Problem

Technology is perhaps the most important material means which serves man as a handmaid in his economic endeavours. It had, however, only very limited role in the creation of cultural activities in the past. With the spectacular developments in technology, it has become a major player in cultural and artistic activities also. Inevitably, material means in the form of technology has emerged as a major player in the production of various cultural products. In the case of music and dancing, two intangible services, for instance, the activity can be stored in a CD and reproduced at a subsequent date with the help of technology. Furthermore, altogether new products with roots in culture, but relying mainly on technology, like that of photography, motion pictures, tele-serials, etc., have also come into existence. The possibility for the reproduction of these cultural products with advanced technology has created an aura of omnipresence around them. In addition, they have acquired the characteristics of mercantile commodities, as they are being produced on factory lines with the help of technology.

Such of those "activities which combine the functions of conception, creation and production of culture with industrial function in large scale manufacture and commercialisation of cultural products" have become the products of some sort of new industrial enterprises[1]. Those enterprises whose products thus encompass industrial and commercial ingredients form what is termed cultural industry. It was a term, coined by Horkheimer Max and Adorno T.W. of the Frankfurt School, which figures as the heading of Chapter 6 of their book *Dialectics of Enlightenment*, published in 1944[2]. The term signifies "the process of industrialisation of the mass produced culture and the commercial imperatives which drove the system"[3]. A number of cultural products are being produced on those lines. Film and television are but two important products of culture industry, which have thus emerged as offshoots of technological advancements. They are novel forms of cultural products, produced and exhibited or transmited with the aid of technology.

In reality, motion pictures and tele-serials are new forms of drama, in which a host of artists participate as in any theatrical performance. The application of highly advanced technology in their creation makes them superior in quality. In the case of dramatic performance in a theatre, the actor appears before the audience. Any flaw in the performance at the time of acting cannot be rectified. On the other hand, dramatic performances in films or television are made in front of camera. Naturally, any defect can be rectified before the product is presented for exhibition or relay. Similarly, make believe situations and dramatic performances can be made more attractive and original with the help of technology. In tele- serial, for instance, "reinforced by the use of a certain elevated acting style, dramatic music and lingering close- up shots, the story lines contain a variety of twists and turns which would stretch the credibility of a realist narrative and that propel the viewer along a roller- coaster ride of emotional ups and downs"[4]. They are produced and reproduced in commodity form at very low unit cost. Naturally, they are able to offer their products at very cheap prices to the audience, the consumer. Thus, they have become rivals to live drama, both from the cultural and economic angles. They could naturally occupy part of the space meant for drama as a cultural product.

The threat from TV in particular is far more serious than from motion pictures. The most important contribution of TV in the realm of art, as mentioned earlier, is the emergence of drama in a new form, termed tele-serial or soap opera. Motion pictures can also be exhibited through television. At the same time, audience can view the programmes by sitting in the privacy of their homes. With these developments, tele-serials manage to appear in the drawing room of each household. In turn, as Raymond Williams enjoins, "most people spend more time watching various kinds of drama than in preparing and eating food"[5]. Apparently, the competition from the mediated drama of culture industry seems to be very stiff.

At the same time, the production of mediated drama calls for very high cost of production on account of heavy dependence on technological inputs. For instance, the total cost of an episode in a tele-serial for half an hour accounts for Rs. 1.5 lakh[6]. On an average, one Malayalam film costs anywhere between Rs. three to five crores[7]. Artists may not be in a position to raise so much capital needed to create such products. Needless to say, moneyed people alone are in a position to produce such products. However, people with money will not bother to produce such cultural products out of charity. Instead, it is profit motive that guides their activities. Culture industry has become a new fertile area potentiality capable of making huge profit. Taking advantage of such favourable conditions, men with money have entered into the field of cultural production in a big way. Standardisation, with an eye on popular appeal becomes the guiding principle with them in the production of cultural goods. Very few among them care to produce works encompassing artistic qualities on account of the lukewarm demand for them. Instead, as

Horkheimer Max and Adorno T.W. enjoin, "the movie makers distrust any manuscript which is not reassuringly backed by best sellers"[8]. Inevitably, the products of culture industry, backed by the superior pulling power, stemming from capital investment eclipse drama as an activity in the market. In the case of television, marketing process itself is being hijacked by the advertisers who make use of the communication potential of television for appealing or persuading the buyers to purchase their own goods. Such intervention invariably results in the supply of the TV serials as a free good. In such a situation, the rational consumer may not take the trouble of going to a theatre and paying the ticket charges to see a dramatic performance. The odds are thus tilted against dramatic theatres in the competitive world. If so, the problem is: can theatrical performance of drama as a cultural activity survive?

The proposal is to uncover the problem by exploring the experience of the dramatic theatres in Kerala which stage Malayalam drama. Kerala has a tradition of different forms of drama for a long period in the past. Some of the important forms of such dramas like *Kathakali* and *Kudiattom* are popular even today. They are religious dramas in ritual forms which could win world wide recognition. The Christians on their part have *Chavittunatakam*, a separate form of artistic performance. Theatrical forms of Malayalam drama of modern period had its origin during the closing decades of the nineteenth century. It was started on the lines of Tamil drama. Subsequently formats of English and Sanskrit dramas were also incorporated. Malayalam drama could shed its dependence on the formats from outside and evolve its own format in course of time. Different formats of drama have been evolved over the years and as on today, Malayalam drama is able to survive with a distinct cultural format of its own.

As an activity relying on the cooperation of a host of artists and other people, dramatic theatres call for institutional support. During the earlier period, it was temples and Christian churches which were providing institutional support. Subsequently, political parties, and social organisations, came forward and organized dramatic performances under their banner. The contributions of KPAC and Kalidasa Kalamandalam in promoting drama in Kerala with political backing are well known. Needless to say, the success of any theatre troupe depends invariably on the dynamism of a director or enterprising artist.

Technologically modified drama of the culture industry began to appear with film making. Film industry could achieve prominence in Kerala since the 1950s. Malayalam ranks fourth among the languages in

India in terms of the number of films produced in a year. Some of the films in Malayalam like Nirmalyam, Swayamvaram, Elipathayam, Kanchana Seetha, etc., were recognized as works of artistic excellence. Cinema is still popular in Kerala inspite of the growing importance of television. TV serials in Malayalam began to appear only since the Asian Games of 1982. However, TV serials in Malayalam, have begun to gain ascendancy after 1996 when Asianet, an exclusive Malayalam channel, was started. In close succession, many channels were started, and programmes in Malayalam began to appear regularly. Evidently, audience can select programmes from any channel with the help of cable system which has penetrated in almost all parts of Kerala around this time.

The emergence of so many channels could exert adverse impact on drama in Malayalam. The channels can relay serials with technical perfection. On the other hand, drama has to be enacted in front of an audience, hailing mainly from the neighbouring localities. With the entry of cinema and serial, a large number of gifted artists have abandoned drama and opted to act in cinema and serials. Apparently, drama has to content with local talents of amateur standard. Furthermore, channels telecast serials for a duration of nearly five hours a day on an average. When as many as fifteen or more channels telecast serials simultaneously, the total output would be for nearly 75 hours a day. Though the so-called "cultural discount" diminishes the competitive strength of non-Malayalam channels, the penetration of non-Malayalam programmes is also fairly widespread in the Kerala market. TV is, therefore, able to colonise much of the time available for leisure activities. In the wake of such colonization of leisure time, a person spends more time in front of the TV than for many other purposes. According to the author's own study, a person spends nearly 13 hours a week for watching TV programmes[9]. Most of the people watch TV during peak hours when serials are aired. It goes without saying that dramas would find it very difficult to withstand the challenge of such a gigantic magnitude from television.

Notwithstanding the apparent penetration of the products of the culture industry, drama in Malayalam seems to hold on. A large number of dramatic clubs and dramatic troupes are active in Kerala. They may not be making any huge volume of profit. Some of the talented artists have moved to films and tele-erials. Even then, dramatic theatres manage to survive. The survival of Malayalam dramatic theatres reminds one of competition between the tortoise and the hare. How they manage to survive is a question requiring serious investigation.

Objectives of the Study

Studies on Malayalam drama are galore. The veteran Malayalam dramatic scholar G. Sankara Pillai, in his work on the history of Malayalam drama, has portrayed the vicissitude of Malayalam drama from its beginning till 1970s[10]. Since television, let alone tele-serial in Malayalam, was yet to appear in Kerala, he was not able to foresee the possible impact of tele-serials on drama. Similarly, Vayala Vasudevan Pillai, in his wide ranging study on Malayalam drama has not touched on the impact of television, though he has covered the development of Malayalam dramas upto to the beginnings of the twenty-first century[11]. Nor has any other author seemed to have attempted to uncover the impact of technological reproduction of drama of the culture industry on Malayalam drama, though some authors like Dhawadker and Mathur have done some preliminary attempts to do the same at the all India level. Nobody seems to be concerned about the deeper implications of the economic parameters on dramatic performances and the travails of drama in the context of the challenges from culture industry. The present study is therefore attempted with the following objectives:

1. To uncover the economic parameters which impinge on dramatic theatres especially in the context of technological innovations;
2. To delineate the complexion of the challenges to Malayalam drama from the technologically mediated dramas like motion pictures and tele-serials of the culture industry;
3. To explore the factors at work in sustaining Malayalam dramatic theatres from the challenge stemming from culture industry and to suggest new policy optons to sustain them.

Concepts and Issues

Concepts suitable for explaining the relation between drama and the products of culture industry and thereby to uncover survival mechanism of drama are galore. To start with, a working definition of dramatic theatres stands foremost for the study as such. Broadly speaking, the definition of theatre as given by Gary Williams seems to be relevant for the study. In his words, "by theatre we usually mean the performances by skilled artists for live audiences, performances that engage the imagination, emotion, intellect and cultural sensibilities of spectators at varying levels"[12]. However, the terms, stage drama and live drama also creep in occasionally in the study with the the same sense as theatrical drama. At the same time, the term theatre which in the usual sense stands for the building and equipment needed for staging a drama also finds references here and there in the study.

Similarly, different forms of performances and even activities are being produced or reproduced with the aid of advanced technology. In such cases, what the technology does is to act or invole as an intermediate agency. When it comes to communication, technology becomes the primary agency of interaction. By itself, drama forms a communication process addressed to the public in live form. Motion pictures or tele-serials are basically, dramatic performances with technology becoming the primary agency of communication. When it comes to the production stage of a motion picture, a technological device, the camera and other instruments come to the picture and act as the facilitating, as well as the recording agency of what transpires in the dramatic communication process. Again, technology becomes the key determinant in the reproduction of the original activity of the performance. Ipso facto, the term technologically mediated drama becomes apt to denote motion pictures and tele-serials. Instead of using the lengthy term, technologically mediated drama, the abbreviated term, mediated drama, is very often used in the study to denote motion pictures and teleserials for the sake of convenience.

The base-superstructure dichotomy which constitutes an important theoretical formulation relating to art can be the starting point to uncover how drama survives the challenge from cultural industry. Cultural activities like drama do not engage in the production of material goods, though the artists have to rely on material means for their subsistence. Accordingly, drama remains as some sort of service activity meant to give expression to creative ideas. As already mentioned, the literary narratives of drama form creative expression par excellence. The literary narrative becomes a reality only when it comes to the performance stage in the theatre. However, as seen earlier, drama is a joint product of a host of artists by which it calls for fairly high cost for each performance. It thus becomes some sort of Janus -faced cultural activity in which "material way of conveyance and intellectual contents to be conveyed" are of equal importance[13]. Needless to say, such activities would be impregnated with both economic and cultural value.

However, norms of the base acquire the upper hand, in the cases relating to the products of the culture industry, as material means represented by advanced technology provide the bulk of the inputs.

Accordingly, culture industry turns out only mercantile commodities meant for making profit. Needless to say, economic parameters come to the fore as people with capital become key players in creating such cultural products. Instead of creating any cathartic effect, they satisfy the entertainment needs of the audience. They are, by and large, meant to draw away all emotional energies from the affairs of real life. One author sarcastically speaks of them as mere pulp art. In the creation or rather production of such works, artistic autonomy is sacrificed at the altar of elevated pleasure. As Horkheimer Max and Adorno. T.W. add, "what is new is not that it is a commodity, but that today it deliberately admits it is one; that art renounces its own autonomy and proudly takes its place among the consumption goods constitutes the charm of novelty"[14]. When they degenerate into a consumption good, they may not be endowed with cultural value which denotes the cultural worth of a product characterised by aesthetic qualities, spiritual values, symbolic significance and historical importance and so on of the transcendental nature.

Unlike the cultural industry per se, dramatic theatres are invariably organised as small units. The amateur dramatic clubs and most of the professional troupes are organised in such manner. Furthermore, many of them are in fact organised as non-profit earning units. A wide variety of artistic activities are being carried by such small units. In the opinion of Throsby such firms strive to create "cultural value subject to both economic and cultural constraints". As he adds further, "the generation of cultural value by non-profit art firms can be portrayed further via an objective function wherein the quality of work produced –and the number of audience reach –are joint maximands, and a break-even financial requirement is entered as the maximum constraint on the generation of economic value"[15]. Some of them which are not able to cover the break-even point may be receiving subsidies from the state or other charitable institutions in order to cover part of the cost of material inputs. The artists themselves may not be receiving any regular remuneration from such units of production for the services rendered by them.

In this connection, the distinction between artists and ordinary labour, as conceptualized by Kant, comes to the fore as another handy concept. Artists who work in culture industry have invariably to forfeit their artistic freedom. Very often, they are downgraded themselves to the status of ordinary labour, as they work only for monetary consideration. On the other hand, artists who are keen to give expression to their creative talents may not behave like a class of mercenary labourers working for money. Their attitude may not be to please anybody and everybody. They are, so to say not audience oriented. Instead, the Tolstoian dictum that the inner need and not external inducement is that, which incites the author to write, holds good squarly with other artists also.

However, such ideal conditions do not exist in the actual world. Most of the artists are not ascetics prepared to lead an austere life. They may seek money not for mere subsistence, but for comfortable living in the form of nutritious food, fashionable clothing, posh housing and other amenities of life. Ipso facto, monetary considerations invariably enter as a powerful factor in their artistic creation also. After taking those realities into consideration, Throsby projects a three-tier model for explaining how monetary consideration enters in the utility function of artists in the creation of artistic value. As he puts, "there are three ways in which income might be entered into our model of creative process: as a constraint, as a joint maximand or as a sole maximand". The first tier stands for those instances where the artist focusses on pure creativity with not a tinge of decision variable affected by economic considerations. As he adds, "the artist is still assumed to be striving solely for the generation of cultural value but within the limitations imposed by the income requirement". This kind of model is applicable to the non-commercial theatre and such other pure artistic enterprises. When it comes to the second tier, both income and financial rewards assume equal importance, so that the objective function of the model can be stated as the joint maximisation of the cultural and economic value arising from the work. Artistic activities which regard creativity as an income earning affair with the cultural value diminishing to zero are on the rise during recent years. Artists occupying the third layer in Throsby's model constitute such category. Most of the films, television programmes and other commercial art fall within the ambit of the third layer[16].

To those artists who intend to continue in their creative endeavours, with little regard to pecuniary gains and also to those who want to gain experience, drama provides a forum for expressing their talents. Some of them may be holding multiple jobs in order to sustain economic viability.

As already mentioned, audiences form an important component in the whole matrix of a drama. In a sense, audiences assume the status of partners in drama. As Dhawadker enjoins, "theatre cannot survive without a community-so long as you are in touch with the needs of a community, your theatre will live, if not it will atrophy and die"[17]. Apparently, how the audience looks at the theatre for the enjoyment of the artistic performance becomes far more important in the survival of drama. Mediated drama on the other hand looks upon audience as mere consumers of a mercantile commodity. In this connection, the distinction between active and passive audience becomes handy for exploring the impact of culture industry on drama. Culture industry on its part regards audience as a weak and helpless class whose weaknesses are exploited by incorporating various ingredients both in the literary style and presentation of the show. However, it is the active audiences who are able to appreciate artistic value and interpret the meaning in a drama, though such class of audience forms only a minority in numerical terms. As a matter of fact, they are those who sustain the drama as a cultural genre from the onslaught of television. The so called "cultural discount" which counts with the audience and which is instrumental in the survival of minority culture throughout the world also comes in the picture[18].

In the light of the aforesaid facts, it can be postulated that drama survives as some kind of Janus-faced artistic activity catering to the tastes of a minority audience in somewhat similar lines as that of poetry. It survives on account of the insistent urge on the part of creative artists to maintain their freedom of expression on the one hand and on the material and moral support of the active audience on the other. In this connection, the issues come to the fore are:

(i) How deep are the involvement of economic parameters in the theatrical dramatic performance and technology mediated dramatic performance of culture Industry respectively?
(ii) Are the products of culture industry superior in quality to that of theatrical drama?
(iii) If not, how does culture industry pose a threat to drama?
(iv) How does dramatic theatres manage to survive in the context of competition from culture industry?
(v) Why do some artists stick on to theatrical drama in thick and thin, even if the remuneration is not very attractive?
(vi) What are the reasons on the part of die-hard audiences to prefer dramas to films and other kinds of mediated drama?
(vii) What should be the policy options for the healthy survival of dramatic theatres?

Methodology

Since the issues call for answers encompassing economic and cultural aspects, investigation relying on a single disciplinary angle may not serve the purpose. Instead, the desirability of a "multi-dimensional and multiperspectival approach to the understanding of television" as advocated by Barker would serve as a meaningful alternative for the current study[19]. Inevitably, divergent methods and approaches cutting across different disciplinary angles with necessary modifications have been adoted to pursue the study.

As a starting point, comparative study of the growth of films and television and how they impinged on drama have been attempted at the macro-level by drawing evidences from various linguistic /country experiences. At the micro-level, a field study on the following lines could gather information about the deeper implication of the threat from the mediated drama to the dramatic theatres and the raisen d'etre for the survival of drama. Accordigly, the magnitude of dramatic theatre units operating in Kerala was enumerated. As a further step, the cost and returns of a few dramatic performances were collected. Needless to say, dramatic units covering up-to the break- even point would be construed as those earning the minimum required for the survival as a firm. While the profit motivated firms seek returns in and above the break even point, the non-profit earning firms would be content in meeting just the break even point. How the units which do not cover the break even point manage to survive was also enquired into. As a further step, the artists and the promoters of the dramatic unit were asked to explain the reasons which prompted them to enter and to adhere steadfastly in the dramatic field, in spite of the seemingly unattractive rate of remuneration in relation to the film world. The field survey was extended to cover the attitude of the audience towards drama as a cultural activity. Many of them would be watching TV also. Why they attended TV was an important question. It was a query posed to them. They were also asked to explain the particular reasons for watching dramas in spite of the difficulties and cost involved in going to the theatres. Their views on the qualities of drama in comparison with the serials was also sought. Answers to most of those questions were sought through open-ended questionnaire.

Data required for the study thus collected form the primary source. Data contained in various publications of official agencies, private researchers and the literature on the subject form the secondary source. Simple stastical methods, like average, percentage etc., seem to be sufficient for analysing the data.

Significance of the Study

What happened to Malayalam dramatic theatres in the wake of

technological advancement in the field of cultural products would be an important area of study from theoretical and practical points of view. While drama, an age old cultural activity, declines in importance, television and films, forming the main components of the mediated drama have grown into gigantic proportions and could attract world wide attention during recent years. The study would be able to shed light on the intricacies of the functioning of culture industry in relation to drama from the experience of Kerala. At the same time, the study would bring to lime light, the contours of cultural economics, an emerging sub-discipline of Economics.

Some forms of art have disappeared over the years in the wake of commodification of art originated with the technological advancement. Similarly, some of them have been marginalised. Yet, some forms of art have benefited immensely with the technological advancement. While uncovering how Malayalam drama could manage to survive the challenge from cultural industry, the study would shed light on the implication of culture industry on the cultural realm of Kerala. The study, it is also hoped, would shed light on the survival strategy of Malayalam dramatic theatres whose position resembles that of the handicrafts which manage to survive in the face of stiff competition from the factory sector.

The policy options to be pursued for safeguarding drama would be formulated on the basis of the study. Preservation of cultural formations and cultural activities are key issues facing the policy makers. While, what is applicable to Malayalam dramatic theatres would also hold good by and large to the dramatic theatres of other languages in India as well. The findings of the study would naturally be relevant to all parts of the country.

NOTES AND REFERENCES

1. Throsby, David (2010); *Economics of Cultural Policy* (Cambridge, University Press) p. 89.
2. The term "Culture Industry" was coined by Adorno, T.W. and Horkheimer Max in their book entitled "Dialectics of Enlightenment" Published in 1944. See James Curran (ed. 1977) *Mass Communication and Society* (London, Open University).
3. Kellner, Douglass (1995); *Media Culture* (London, Routledge) p. 28.
4. Barker Chris (1997); *Global Television: An Introduction* (Oxford, Blackwel Publishers) p. 79.
5. Williams Raymond (1975); *Television: Technology and Cultural Form* (London, Routledge) p. 60.

6. Joseph, K.V. (2010); *Economics of Culture Industry: Television in India* (New Delhi, Shipra Publications) p. 78
7. www.dnaindia.com/entertainment/report
8. Horkheimer Max and Adorno. T.W; *op. cit.,* p. 357.
9. Joseph, K.V. (2010); *op. cit.,* p. 155.
10. Pillai G. Sankara (1970); *Malayala Nataka Sahithya Charithram* (Mal) History of Malayalam Drama (Thrissur, Kerala Sahitya_Academy).
11. Pillai Vayala Vasudevan (2005); *Malayala Nataka Sahithya Charithram* (Mal) History of Malayalam Drama (Thrissur, Kerala Shitya Academy).
12. Williams Gary Jay (2010); *Theatre Histories: An Introduction* (New York Routledge, Taylor and Francis Group) P, Preface XX.
13. Burger, Anna (1970); *Economic Problems of Consumer Services* (Budapest, Akademai Kiado) p. 41.
14. Horkheimer Max and Adorno. T.W. *op. cit.,* p. 367.
15. Throsby David 2001); *Economics and Culture* (Cambridge, University Press) p. 117.
16. See Throsby David (2001); *op. cit.*, pp. 96-102.
17. Dharwadker, Arpana Bhargava (2005); *Theatres of Independence Drama, Theory, and Urban Performance in India since 1947* (Oxford University Press) p. 100.
18. The concept "Cultural Discount" stands for the preference of any particular linguistic or cultural group to the cultural products of their own products. see Joseph. K.V. (2000); *Economics of Culture Industry: Television in India (Delhi, Shipra, Publications)* p. 120.
19. Barker Chris (1997); *Global Television: An Introduction* (Oxford, Blakwell Publishers) p. 6.

2

Evolution of Dramatic Theatres over the Years

In the previous Chapter, the various issues cropping up in the realm of drama with the entry of technologically mediated drama were spelt out. Almost all societies had some sort of dramatic performance from ancient past. Drama in its present form is the outcome of changes in its format stretching back to centuries. In this Chapter, the focus is on how drama evolved over years as a fusion of economics and artistic genres preceded by a brief introduction of the important characteristics of drama.

Characteristics of Drama

The term drama originates from the Greek word *dreon,* meaning doing. Similarly, the word theatre originates from the Greek word *theatron* meaning seeing. Theatres are the loci where visible dramatic actions are performed. If so, what exactly are the actions performed which can be seen in theatre. ? They are imitations of events superimposed by spectacles accompanied by verbal expressions, very often expressed in symbolic form termed drama. The term drama itself is used in two senses. In the first place, it stands for a literary piece of work as in the case of a novel or epic. As a literary piece of art, drama denotes "a story devised to be presented by actors on a stage before an audience"[1]. The literary piece which is termed the script is composed by an author depicting a series of events connected to each other as in the case of a novel or other forms of narrative art, provides the basic structure of a drama. The arrangement of events in the narrative form is otherwise known as the plot. Unlike other forms of narratives, drama is designed in such a way as to be enacted by the actors in front of an audience. It acquires a concrete shape, when it is enacted by a band of actors invariably in a theatre. The enactment of drama stands for the second sense in which the term drama is used. In other words, it denotes the live performance of drama in a theatre as designed by an author. Thus it relies on a "two fold foundation, mimetic-dramatic art and literary dramatic art"[2].

However perfect it is as a literary work, the quality of dramatic performance depends on the histrionic skill and dedication to work on the part of actors. What the playwright does is to narrate a story in such a way as to be presented by actors. The dramatist is obviously at the mercy of the actors for its quality as a work of art. If any of the actors and other artists fail to convey the message that the dramatist intended, the dramatist will fail in his intention, though the fault is not his own. A most delicate love scene can be spoiled by an actor, incapable of emotional expression. The success of Miller, a brilliant director, stems, as Hamilton lauds, "by sheer visual imagination, in the setting and handling of the stage, especially in the first act and the last. Mr. Miller, contrived to endow the author's shallow fabric with the semblance of reality"[3]. Similarly, good actors can end as mere flops by the incompetence of the director. At the same time, good actors are invariably in a position to produce excellent dramatic works as Molire or Shakespeare did. They were also talented playwrights. However gifted, writers need not necessarily be good playwrights. In England for example, great poets like Scott, Coleridge, Byron, Shelly, Keats, Browning, Mathew Arnold, Tennyson, etc., had tried their luck as dramatists with little success in producing any dramatic work of good quality. Drama is not merely the mimetic act of a play, but also an embodiment of other equally important artistic ingredients. It lavishly makes use of arts like music, dance, painting, decoration and spectacle. As Esslin adds, "In drawing on the other arts and fusing them into a new whole, drama thus is the most hybrid—or the most complete synthesis of all the arts"[4],

Unlike other forms of art, drama bestows special attention to the audience. At the same time, drama is the only art, excepting oratory and certain forms of music, with an appeal primarily to a crowd rather than to an individual. In fact, most of the other forms of art, are basically meant to satisfy the author himself. On the other hand, drama will not be able to command attention as a work of art, unless it is addressed to an audience. A good dramatist who knows the mob psychology can alone address them in the language known to them with the ideas which they can understand. Dramatists like Shakespeare, who wrote plays to the masses, could appeal with ease to "the basic common place emotions like love of women, love of country, love of right, anger, jealousy, evenge, ambition, lust, treachery, etc., than the sublime ideals of life"[5]. The audiences who come to see a drama themselves become partisans in their attitude, like the spectators who watch football match or cricket series.

Dramas are broadly divided into tragedies and comedies. The theme of any drama is the struggle for life in various manifestations. However, the theme of tragic drama is on a struggle foredoomed to fail because the individual human being is pitted against forces stronger than himself. According to Aristotle, the founding father of dramatic theory, "tragedy then is an imitation of an action that is serious, complete, and of a certain magnitude; in language embellished with each kind of artistic ornament, the several kinds being found in separate parts of the play; in the form of action, not of narrative; through pity and fear effecting the proper purgation of these emotions"[6]. Tragedy itself is divided into tragedy proper and melodrama. In both, a set of characters struggle vainly to avert a predetermined doom. While in a tragedy, the characters determine and control the plot, in melodrama, the plot determines and control the characters. Unlike tragedy, merri-mooded drama falls within the category of comedy. They are of two kinds, comedy proper and farce. A comedy is a humorous play in which the actors dominate the action, whereas in a farce, though humorous by itself, action dominates the actors, the ambit of comedy.

Unlike other forms of art, drama which is a cooperative effort of different forms of art, requires different kinds of material inputs on a fairly large scale. A theatre required for staging the performance and accommodating the audience for conveniently watching the programme is perhaps the most important material input. The theatre has to be decorated. Similarly, the artists have to be dressed with proper attire, ornaments and make- up materials. Progress in technology has added new dimensions in the application of various inputs in the dramatic performance. The theatre itself is being equipped with electric fittings, sound system, etc., for making it more attractive. Even acting is being made more realistic and attractive by utilising various technological devices.

Being a cooperative activity, drama requires the service of an organisation for staging and reaping any economic benefit. The organisation known as the theatre or theatre troupe marshalls various inputs like the theatre, the artists, the ordinary labour, etc., without the active involvement of which drama per se, cannot be enacted. In so doing, it becomes as much an economic activity, as an artistic activity. (Further reference on this aspect will be made elsewhere.)

Origin of Drama

The origin of drama can be traced to the inherent urge of man for imitation. In the words of Aristotle, "imitation is implanted in man from childhood, one difference between him and other animals being that he is the most imitative of living creatures and through imitation learns his earliest lessons, and no less universal is the pleasure felt in things imitated."[7]. From the urge for imitation, he has successfully introduced, by degrees, dance, magic and ritual ceremonies, the different variations of imitation in concrete form. As Aristotle adds further, "next there is the instinct for harmony and rhythem, metres being manifestly sections of rhythm. Persons, therefore, starting with this natural gift developed, by degrees, their special aptitudes, till their rude improvisations gave birth to poetry". The improvisation of poetry by degrees led to the emergence of drama "a larger and higher form of art", as Aristotle describes it.

Ancient Period

Drama in the concrete form which had its origin in Athens is believed to have evolved as an offshoot of the festival of Dionysus, the god of fertility, held every year during Jan to March. The festival used to commence with a procession to the temple accompanied by dance and music known as dithyramb by different bands of chorus in honour of Dionysus. In course of time, dithyramb was performed in honour of other heroes. Subsequently, dramatic performance in the form of tragedy was introduced as part of the festival. The word tragedy originated from the word *tragos,* meaning, goat and *ode* meaning music. It is the symbolic of the killing of the goat in the altar as a sacrifice to the deity and singing in praise of the god or hero. According to legend, Thespis who lived around the sixth century B.C., is credited with having introduced tragedy in the midst of dithyramb, during the festival in 534 B.C. In the course of time, other play wrights appeared and perfected tragedies as an art. Mythological stories of Greeks were invariably adopted as the theme of tragedies. It became a practice in course of time to make competition of tragedies during the festival which lasted for five days. On the first day, there was the procession of the deity. Dithyramb was performed on the second day. Third, fourth and fifth days were earmarked for competition of tragedies. The drama adjudged as the best was awarded prizes. Euripides, Sophocles and Aeschylus were identified as the leading figures in writing and staging tragedies in Athens during the fifth century B.C. Among them, Aeschylus is said to have written ninety plays, Sophocles well over hundred, and Euripedes ninety-two plays altogether, nearly one century after the days of Thespis. Excepting 33, all of them have disappeared. Among them, *Oedipus Rex* of Sophocles stands as an outstanding Greek tragedy. Competitions of comedies, and farce were introduced subsequently. Aristophanes, the originator of comedies and Menander who wrote domestic farce, or satire lived around this time and presented them during the competition. Thus the three forms of drama, viz., tragedy, comedy and satire were written and staged.

Actors were few in numbers with men alone appearing on the stage. With voice as the great asset, the Greek actor was primarily a speaker rather than an actor of the modern sense[8]. In those days, Athens remained the theatrical capital of Greek world and audience from all over Greece used to attend the annual festival. Admission to the theatre was free. Later, when there was a small charge, tickets were given to those who could not afford to buy them. The state paid the actors, but the cost of physical production of each play was met by a rich citizen, who was then honoured with the title of *choragus*[9]. Apparently, from the formative days, the existence of an economic dimension existed as an integral part of dramatic performances. The budgeted cost of the festival including drama accounted for 40 talents per year "(about 3/4 million dollars on our conversion scale)"[10]. However, the dramatic festivals were made possible by a two-part system of subsidy involving generous grants by the state and the lavish contributions of the private citizens which was theoretically voluntary but "enforced by law and custom"[11].

Since drama was introduced in the midst of choral recitations, chorus remained as an integral part of drama. During the period of Thespis chorus comprised fifty persons. Aeschylus reduced it to twelve. Sophocles raised it to fifteen. For any performance the actors consisted of three persons. They covered their head invariably with a mask. Actors were highly gifted persons. As Macgowan and Melnitz observe, "the Greeks venerated them as servants of Dionysus, exempted them from military duty and sometimes entrusted them with diplomatic and political missions"[12]. The theatre itself was in the premises of the temple of Dionysus at the foot of Acropolis, which was located in a narrow space of land in between two hills. Accommodation was provided to the audiences at the slopes of the hills, and the actual stage was at the bottom of the hill. A proper theatre of Dionysus which could accommodate some 15000 to 20000 spectators, was actually built around 340 B.C. only[13].

While the Athenian dramatists of the fifth century B.C. were instrumental in writing outstanding dramatic works, it was Aristotle, the Greek philosopher who provided a theoretical base for drama as an art. He devoted the first four chapters of his *Poetics* to explain the nature and virtue of Greek drama. The three unities-unity of time, place and action, of dramatic plays have been associated with Aristotle, in addition to his having introduced the famous cathartic effect of tragedies.

The Romans who succeeded the Greeks in the political realm, had no theatrical tradition as that of the Greeks. During the Republican period, Rome maintained strict puritan standards towards public theatre and accordingly dramatic activities were looked upon with contempt. Only after the emergence of the Empire, theatres could gain credibility in the Roman World. The first theatre was constructed by Pompey in B.C. 55. Subsequently, Colosseum, which became the seat of bloody entertainments of the Romans, and theatres in other parts of the empire came up.

Nevertheless, they had their own dramatic festivals which were called *ludi*, or games, because they were devoted mainly to sports and amusements such as boxing and rope dancing. At first, the *ludis were* held in April, July, September and November, every year, but later, on the occasions like that of a military triumph, or the funeral of an important citizen. In course of time, farcical performances crept in from provinces[14]. However, theatre became mere show business. As an authority enjoins, "the actor manager had his troupes of slaves, freedmen and foreigners. He bought a play outright from its author or adapter, paid for the costumes and properties and assumed all the risks of production and presentation. If the play proved popular, he was given money in proportion to its success, and sometimes a prize of palm leaves or a crown of silver or gold"[15]. The games and plays were in the same theatre which became bloodier and more violent. The most popular dramatic entertainments in the Empire were pantomimes that used music and dance costumes and settings to retell Greek myths.

Rome is credited with having its own dramatists. Prominent among them were Seneca, Terence and Plautus. Though some of them like Seneca wrote original scripts, most of them translated or adapted Greek plays. Comedies, rather than tragedies were popular in the Roman world. In sum, as an authority observes, "the theatre was too common and degraded an institution in the eyes of the learned and well placed"[16].

Middle Ages

The Graeco-Roman dramatic tradition was on the path of decline with the fall of the Empire and the rise of Christianity. In fact, Christianity was hostile to the entire dramatic heritage of the so- called pagan period. Christians shunned the theatre which was labelled as the Church of the devil. In the fifth century, actors were even denied communion in the church[17]. However, gradually, the Church came forward to promote and encourage dramatic art, as it could be suitably used for instilling religious teachings. Accordingly, they promoted dramatic themes impregnated with Biblical stories, Christian legends and endeavours of Christian heroes[18]. The performances fostered by Church were known as mystery and miracle plays. Initially, almost all the players were priests and religious men. Later on, laymen also began to play in them. In course of time, these plays spread through the agency of bards and troubadours that wandered from court to court of the feudal barons[19]. Since the mystery plays were dull and monotonous, "interludes", which were nothing other than mere slapstick farces, noted for their vulgarity, instead of humour, started to appear gradually. Apparently, the Church was unable to stamp out completely the festive spirit among the common people.

Actors were getting fairly attractive remuneration in those days. In England, for example, a "man received three shillings and four pence 'for pleayng God', another man four pence, for hanging Judas, and one shilling for playing Noah"[20]. Furthermore, in course of time, it became a standard practice to charge an entrance fee to watch the miracle plays, apparently as the staging of the plays became costly[21]. Nevertheless, the ratings of theatre remained very poor during the greater part of the Middle Ages. "There were no theatres for practical purposes, and the wandering actors would hardly have graced the carnivals and burlesque shows"[22]. For almost two thousand years, the theatre of Europe lay dead. "Between 400 B.C. to the close of 1600, no dramatist wrote a single great play and the stage was barren"[23].

Onset of Renaissance

With the Renaissance which heralded with the fall of Constantinople to the Turks in 1453, there was a reawakening of the artistic and dramatic activities. It was rendered possible with the plight of the scholars from Greece to the Western Europe with scholarly works of ancient Greek and Roman authors. In close succession, scripts and dramatic performances on the ancient model began to appear in Italy, Spain, France and England. Play houses and theatres also sprang up in different parts of Europe.

Such changes in social and cultural life, ensued wth the arrival of scholars from Greece is known as the Renaissance.

As a starting point, interludes, which deviated from the mystery plays of didactic value, moved further by incorporating music and dance as part of the show. In close succession satirical plays, presenting historical themes in dramatic form were also on the anvil. Works on the models of classical Latin plays, very often in the native vernacular script began to appear. Furthermore, both tragedies and comedies on the lines of classical Greek and Latin scripts were soon to appear. Works of Plautus and Terence, which were hidden in the monasteries, were rediscovered and enacted with enthusiasm.

The Renaissance started first in Italy. One of the important steps taken up by Italians during the Renaissance period was the construction of theatres on the models of classical Latin theatres. Teatro Farnese of Parma was one of the earliesrt theatres, followed by Teatro Olimpico in Vicenza[24]. Some of them manage to survive even today as monumental structures. Credit should also go to Italy for having produced excellent paintings, sculptures and architecture during the Renaissance. It was in Italy wherein stage decoration was introduced for the first time. Opera was also introduced by them during that period. However, Italy seems to have produced no play of lasting standards. One reason for this seems to be the lack of a dedicated audience, ready to sustain dramatic performances with the material support through the payment of admission fee. The Italian audiences in those days were never the vigorous and imaginative class that sustained drama similar to that of Spain at the time of Lopez de Vega in Spain, or Shakespeare, in England[25]. Nevertheless, troupes of Italian comedians and actors managed to tour in Spain, France, and even England and won laurels[26],

The situation was altogether different in Spain, where some of the finest dramatic pieces were written during the period of Renaissance. Cervantes, the author of Don Quixote, was one of the prominent dramatists of Spain. Though he was a prodigious author, he was thrust into jail because of his financial imprudence, and in the end, he died in poverty. The next important author, Lopez de Vega, was equally gifted with his writings as well as in real life. He was the inventor and pioneer of the golden age of Spanish drama and accordingly, he was called the prodigy of nature. Calderon regarded as the last of the notable Spanish playwrights conquered both court and populace. As many as 200 comedies and autos were produced by him. Strolling players toured throughout Spain even after permanent theatres were built. Theatrical companies in Spain were bound to share their income with hospitals and charity institutions. Admission prices varied from place to place. In 1575, the general admission was half a real, an arm-chair seat on the lower floor cost one real more and a box office seat six reales (one real was equivalent to 12.5 cents)[27]. The playwright used to sell his work outright. The best could get perhaps 300 reales for an auto and 550 reales for a comedia.

According to Maugham, drama, at no time, and in no country, has flourished so luxuriantly as in Spain, during the hundred years that ended with Calderon's death. By 1681, there were as many as forty theatres in Madrid and with well over 2000 actors in the rolls. It is estimated that well over 30000 plays were written and performed with some of them reckoned as world famous works, even today[28].

The Renaissance which had its beginnings in Italy eventually, spread to England where the receptivity to it was warm from the very beginning. In fact, scholars and poets from England flocked into Italy to learn humanism and the classics. On their return to England they introduced play writing and play acting in universities, law schools and even in schools. The students were called upon to compose dramatic works and to enact them in schools as part of their curriculum. Interestingly, even the award of degree was contingent upon the writing of comedies and acting them. Very often, students and lawyers brought their plays to the queen in the palace. The comedies which they wrote were in native English. *Gorboduc,* the first full length tragedy in English tongue, came out in 1560. Significantly, most of the dramatists were alumni of Cambridge or Oxford.

While choir boys and school boys and students at universities and lawyers at the Inns of Courts were producing plays, professional actors were far from idle. On the village greens and in banquet halls, and inn yards, they were giving shows, though crude at times, but were popular. The players attached to the noble households were also busy with shows and performances. Some of them played even in London. James Burbage, built the first theatre, in which Shakespeare was one among the earlier partners. Around the middle of the century, touring troupes were still playing mysteries and moralities. Chronicle forming another genre, became popular just before Queen Elizabeth assumed the throne. During 1580s about a dozen chronicle plays, and in the nineties of the 16th century nearly eighty were produced. It was in those ten years that playwrights of skill and resource came to the London theatre. Shakespeare was one among them who appeared in the scene with his works *Henry VI* and *Richard 11* in 1590[29].

The last half of Queen Elizabeth's reign witnessed many extraordinary developments. A new kind of playhouse designed by James Burbage was one among them. Christopher Marlowe, the first great dramatist, with his *Tamburlaine* appeared in the scene in 1587. Within fifteen years London saw Shakespeare's *Richard 111, The Taming of the Shrew, Romeo and Juliet, A Midsummer Night's Dream, Julius Caesar, Hamlet, etc.* Shakespeare became very popular and one dramatist jocularly called him the "upstart crow"[30]. Ben Jonson, though a rival to Shakespeare, but magnanimously declared that, Shakespeare "was not of an age but for the time"[31]. Nevertheless, the economic impulses seem to have been very strong with Shakespeare. As Hamylton adds, "he was a careful money-making businessman fond of food and drink and of outdoors—"[32]. The Queen and her nobles respected Shakespeare with the same enthusiasm as the common people and whenever the queen could not go to the public playhouses, she saw his plays at court or in the players inns. Besides Shakespeare, an array of eminent dramatists had contributed their share in a bigway and elevated English drama to an exalted position during the time of Queen Elizabeth. Starting with Marlowe, the galaxy included Ben Jonson, Thomas Heywood, William Kempe, Richard Burbage, Richard Tarlton, etc. Some of them like Shakespeare or Ben Jonson were dramatists as well as actors.

A typical Elizabethan play-house stood roofless in the air. The stage was a projecting platform surrounded, on three sides, by the groundlings, or "the pit", as it was then known. Boxes for city madams and the gentlemen of means were built around the pit. At the back of the platform was hung an arras through which the players entered. No scenery was employed. Since there was no curtain, the actors could never be discovered on the stage and were forced to make an exit at the end of every scene. Plays were staged by daylight invariably in the afternoon with no darkening of the stage[33]. Play-houses were of two types: the public and private. While public play houses were large outdoor theatres, the private ones were smaller indoor theatres. The capacity of a public play house was for about an audience of 3000, and the private playhouses could accommodate only 700. At the public theatre, majority of the spectators had to stand on the dirty mud floor for a penny, and the remaining could get accommodation in the galleries or boxes. In the private theatres, the spectators had to pay six pence or more for sitting accommodation[34].

Actors used to form companies of their own to stage performance. When the Globe and Fortune flourished, there were about twenty well balanced companies of skilled and respected players[35]. The typical company employed eight to twelve performers. Significantly, companies of players invariably had to secure the patronage of a noble man, if they wanted to tour in comparative safety. Patronage became the standard of the day as kings and earls used to keep a troupe of actors among their household servants out of vanity as it could spread their name across the countryside. Some of them retained a troupe of actors for entertaining the nobles and members of the household. It was a mark of status for royal and ducal courts to patronise and to house a comedia troupe[36]. The actors, in turn, were benefited by reflected glory. "The role of patron was primarily the protection of the actors from harassment "as Roges, Vacabondes and Sturdy Beggars" and no benefits other than prestige and suits of clothing – seem to have accrued"[37]. The companies used to pass from one noble man to another. The death of patrons, defection among the actors, and the calamitous plagues that erupted from time to time disrupted old companies and paved the way for the creation of new companies[38]. In many cases, the financial and theatrical business was in the hands of stock companies formed by some ten to fifteen players, who would buy shares at about seventy pounds. The capital so raised went mainly for plays and costumes. They had to pay fairly big amount as theatre rent. The sharers used to hire other actors at six pence a week. The lads who played women's part were apprenticed by the company and were paid a few shillings per week. The companies in London rented theatres from their owners. They were entitled for the money collected at the gate. The money collected at the gate was dropped through a slot in a box from which the term box office has originated[39]. Thus theatrical enterprise then, was essentially an "unsubsidized commercial venture"[40]. Nevertheless, the dramatic companies used to receive 10 pounds for a performance at the court or at the home of the barons which was slightly more than what they could normally get as gross income from a performance in its own theatre[41]. Many of the companies were not able to meet both ends, though some of them were able to earn substantial amount of profit. It is reported that on an average, one out of eight Londoners used to go to the theatre once in a week during the period of Shakespeare[42]. Even then, the bulk of the theatre-going people belonged to upper classes. The ordinary people were interested in other forms of entertainments like, "cock fighting, boxing, and other popular entertainments"[43].

During those years, playwriting alone was not sufficient to make a living. Plays were sold for six to eight pounds. Some playwrights used to get a portion of the profits from the second or third performance of their plays. Interestingly, the total income of Shakespeare from the sale of his plays was probably only about 300 pounds. Because of the generosity of Burbage, his colleague, Shakespeare had for many years not only his salary as a player, but also a share in the profit of the company. He owned one of the ten shares of the Globe, the dramatic company with which he was associated[44].

Unlike Spain or Italy or England, dramatic performances were slow to develop in France. Staging of mystery plays in open fields, public squares, Roman amphitheatres, palaces and even cemeteries continued to persist there, right throughout the Middle Ages. Nevertheless, Hotel de Bourgogne, which is perhaps the first public playhouse of Europe since the fall of Rome was constructed in 1550. However, a second theatre had to wait till 1634. Similarly, it was only after 1637 that France could be credited with having notable native playwrights[45]. It seems that the monopoly control of Confrerie, a company of amateur actors, with exclusive privilege for producing plays since 1402, stood in the way of staging dramas or even forming dramatic troupes. Even touring companies gave only fly-by-night performances to escape from prosecution from Confrerie. Plays at fairs were legalised only by an edict of 1595. It was Cardinal Richelieu who was instrumental in abolishing the monopoly and paved the way for the emergence of dramatic activities in France. He himself became a playwright, very often in collaboration with some other authors. There were court theatres, which delighted kings and courtiers in balls, ballets and spectacles. King Louis XIV showered encouragement to all forms of performances for his courtiers and their ladies. In addition, he gave goodly subsidies to the Italian players, and to Moliere. As in England, classic drama became part of curriculum in colleges in France also. Many of the playwrights were teachers of rhetoric with most of the works written in the native language, the French.

The belated entry was made good by the contribution of a galaxy of playwrights and artists. The first among them was Hardy, who wrote tragedies, tragic-comedies, melodramas and pastorals. All in all, he, according to some, wrote as many as 1200 pieces. Another one was Racine, who wrote mainly tragedies. The outstanding dramatist of France was Moliere, whose scripts were mainly comedies. The comic genius of Moliere dominated the French dramatic world during his life time. Actors in France who could command credentials became heads of dramatic companies. Royal patronage to drama was strong especially during the period of Louis XIV.

Theatre prices varied from play to play and the position of seating arrangements. A law of 1609 limited them to five sous, but by the middle of the century a place in box at the Bourgogne cost 110 sous and at the end, the best seat at the Guegnaud or Comedie-francaise cost seven francs and four sous. Prices were lowered whenever the plays lost popularity. The sale of lemonade, brought additional income to the theatres (20 sous equal 2 shillings and 2 pense)[46]. Acting companies were set up as in England on a sharing basis. Each actor contributed a fixed amount of capital at the beginning and could not be discharged before the end of a definite period of time. Actors who wrote a play received an extra share during its early performances. A playwright who is not an actor might be given a share or part of a share. State support was one of the pillars in the sustenance of the theatres during this period. Throughout the Renaissanc period, France failed to create free and imaginative dramatic works as in England or Spain, though the genius of Moliere broke the bounds of a rigid verse form and a narrow social environment[47].

In England, dramatic activities could not maintain the Elizabethan legacy during the years following the death of the Queen. In the wake of the Puritan hegemony of the Commonwealth period, drama itself was banned. Nevertheless, wandering actors "used to act privately at three or four miles, or more, out of town, now here, sometimes in noblemen's houses"[48]. Significantly, it was during this period that female actresses appeared for the first time on the English stage, though their performance in operas were allowed to function earlier in lieu of other theatrical performances[49]. Even after the Restoration, theatres could not regain their past glory.

In the Restoration theatre, the pit, or the main floor, had benches and the price of admission was two shillings and sixpence. There were usually two big galleries of one shilling and six pence and the one shilling prices were often doubled for the first performance of new plays. Production technique was rather simple. There were back drops that could be raised or lowered and there was a front curtain often painted with a scene. Performances used to start in the early afternoon because the streets were not safe after dark. Costuming was a problem from financial point of view, and it is reported that the king lent his coronation robes for one play and the dukes made similar loans[50]. Similarly, in 1667, the king gave 500 pounds for sixteen scarlet robes for the production of Catiline.

Renaissance was slow to reach the Germanic soil, mainly on account of internal wars and the absence of a unified political authority. Nevertheless, Germanic people had a native form of comedy, distinct from the Holy drama of the Middle Ages. It was a carnival play known as Shrovetide, with full of horseplay and even ribaldry. These were indigenous artifacts poking fun at local people and lampooning the burghers who ruled the community. A favourite character was the Narr which typified the earthy beer drinking German jokester. The carnival plays dealt with human frailties such as avarice, infidelity, gluttony, and brought the offenders and victims alike to a mock court. These farces were staged by amateurs who set in rude stages in a public hall, or village square and offered free entertainment. Later on, companies known as Meistersingers by group of actors and vocalists were established[51]. Surprisingly, companies of English, French and Italian actors were entertaining Germans before the end of the Thirty Year War.

As in other parts of Europe, German women were also precluded from appearing in dramatic plays. However, it was through a woman that the German stage could acquire dignity and status. She was Frederika Carolina Neuber who joined a theatrical troupe in 1717 and continued to dominate the dramatic field of Germanic world till the end of her life. Unfortunately, she died in poverty, apparently on account of her weakness for extravagant stage display[52]. The men who elevated German drama to a pinnacle of glory were Schiller and Goethe who wrote dramatic works and directed theatres of their own. Financial support from the Duke of Weimer became handy in sustaining their efforts. The romantic movement which took shape at a later date was inspired by the works of Schiller and Goethe. Though romantic movement is associated with the leading writers of the day, it could not make its imprint in the dramatic field. In the words of H.G. Wells, "it meant instinct against reason and emotion against science—It was opposed not only to the realities of the present but to the classic past"[53].

Developments during Nineteenth Century

Western countries witnessed a series of events having wider implications on dramatic theatres like wars, political upheavals, industrial revolution, urbanisation etc., during the 19th and 20th centuries. Most of the creative minds sought for change and betterment in their endeavours. Play goers and theatres grew in number when the era of industrial development ushered in. However, the bulk of the new audiences was uneducated who looked to the stage as an escape from the world in which they lived and worked. Acting advanced from bravura display of star talent to well rehearsed ensembles and to a natural style of acting that suited the realistic play. Technology provided the stage with gas, limelight, and finally with incandescent bulb[54]. Taking advantage of such favourable conditions, profit seeking entrepreneurial classes endeavoured to make gains by staging performances which could meet the entertainment needs of the growing working class who congregated in the urban centres. Thus an era of pure commercialisation in the field of dramatic theatres became a reality.

Playwrights moved from classicism to romanticism and to realism. While a few moved toward poetic, some moved very close to expressionism. Another significant development was the entry of the new stage play of Ibsen and Bjornson, two giants from the Scandinavian countries, who opened new paths in the direction of realism in drama. Towards the end, both of them emphasized on spiritual rather than materialist values in their realistic plays. Deeper character analysis formed another distinguishing characteristic of Ibsen's works[55]. Strindberg another stalwart from Scandinavia, who started his career with historical plays, took up realism and finally turned to a form which might be called symbolic interpretation of actuality which became the forerunner of expressionism[56]. Interestingly, an author, Sean O'Casey humorously compared Ibsen and Strindberg thus: "Ibsen can sit serenely in his doll's house, while Strindberg is battling with heaven and hell"[57]. Among the British dramatists Bernard Shah remains the tallest, notwithstanding the presence of a galaxy of dramatists like Oscar Wilde, John Galsworthy, and Somerset Maugham. In fact, many of them could attain only the status of authors of closet dramas.

Growth of Dramatic Theatres in the US

While European scene was brisk with the creation of new formats and genres, the United States of America, which was destined to become the citadel of technologically mediated drama in the years to come, was lukewarm, if not hostile, towards dramatic activities, mainly on account of the Puritan tradition of the original British Colonies which formed the nucleus of the future United States. As there was a shortage of actors, it was the actors from England and other European countries who toured and entertained people with theatrical performance in various parts of the US. While most of them, returned to Europe after acting in a few dramas, some of them opted to stay in the US as permanent citizens. Well organised troupes also occasionally visited America and staged plays there. When the American war of Independence started, actors from England became suspects and interestingly, the Company of London Comedians changed its name as The American Company of Comedians to escape the wrath of the public[58]. Subsequently, theatrical companies were formed by actor businessmen, and enrolled troupes of actors by paying fixed rates of remuneration. Construction of a few theatres of moderate scale was also in the offing. It took a boost with the construction of Park, a massive theatrical structure in 1798 at a cost of $130,000 with a capacity to hold 2000 spectators[59]. Eventually, theatres sprang up in other cities. At that time, actors' salaries ranged from $4 to $50 a week, with the visiting stars getting as much as $100. The total cost for running the shows per week was about $1161. Prices of admission remained at about twenty-five cents to a dollar in those days[60]. Apparently, dramatic activities were organized on pure commercial lines in the USA from the formative days.

There were only very few theatres in the US in 1800. Since then, the American stage started to expand with the growth of population of the country. By 1885, there were well over 5000 play-houses and in between 50000 and 70000 players against hardly 150 actors in 1800 when America had no actor who could be rated as star[61]. The ongoing inflow of stars from England was still in progress. In 1810, the Park theatre in New York brought a leading star, George Frederic Cooke from England. The Park paid his passage, guaranteed him a salary of twenty -five guineas (a little more than 25 pounds) for each of ten months and twenty-five cents a mile for travelling expenses on tour[62]. The touring system continued to flourish high in popularity till towards the close of the nineteenth century. A Broadway hit or a well known star could play in hundreds of theatres over almost 100,000 miles of railroad. Nevertheless, good acting companies held sway in the metropolitan cities[63].

The US scenario exhibits a few distinguishing characteristics. As stated earlier, there was expansion in the number of dramatic theatres and companies, with the star becoming the focal point of attraction. Commercial interest became the driving force behind theatrical dramas. However, America could not produce any lasting dramatic play of artistic qualities. Nor any dramatist could grow in stature as an outstanding artist.

Developments in Stage Arrangements.

Stage arrangements were rather poor for a long period in the past. Even performances were staged in the open ground during the heyday of Greek drama. Permanent theatres began to come up after the construction of the theatre of Dionysus in the year 340 BC. Stage arrangement capable of attracting and at the same time, suitable for providing amenities to the audience was on the anvil from the nineteenth century onwards. The era of extravaganza in staging also became visible. As an author says, "the embrace limits that had fuelled the imagination of earlier dramatists had been eclipsed by the fascination for decorative effect"[64]. Such developments, in the arena of stage craft with much more vigour was in the offing in the years to follow. Adolph Appia of Switzerland and Edward Gorden Craig of Great Britain set in motion a revolution in the designing and lighting of scenery. An Austrian born director, Max Reinhardt supplemented what the earlier stalwarts did. The nineteenth century type of scenery which was then in vogue had been invented nearly two hundred years back, was suited mainly to the the opera. Appia's basic aim was to strengthen, "the dramatic action". This was to be done not only through the setting, but quite as much through the lighting. He was not interested to put up an exciting visual show. He wanted to serve the actor. As he puts, "It is the presence of the actor, upon the stage which causes dramatic action. Without the actor there would be no action". For this purpose, he wanted a plastic or three dimensional set, because the actor had that quality and the actor's movements could only have meaning in relation to obstacles and point of support offered to it by ground and the natural objects". This made Appia, to design a setting that had a kind of solid reality, as well as various levels for the actor to work upon. However, he recognised that the three-dimensional construction could not solve by itself the obvious conflict between a living actor and a dead setting. He felt that they must be united and dramatised by light. He wanted a living light by lighting on the stage to change with the passage of time; or to change in a way that threw the action of the play into sharper relief. In his writings, he showed how the effect of the setting, the showing actor and the changing lights would follow and thereby heighten the course of action[65].

Craig went further and maintained that the "theatre should not be a place in which to exhibit scenery,—it should be a place in which the entire beauty of life can be unfolded—the inner beauty and the meaning of life". He recognised that the theatre is a synthesis of many arts and many skills. It is not merely the play or acting, scenery, light, music, movement or dance. The theatre combines all or most of those things. In his opinion, production must be a clean and clear fusion of settings, costumes, movement and perhaps music, so that the acting may present the play in its fullest effect[66].

On the other hand, the European plays and productions after the First World War veered away from the realistic concept. They followed a path leading to a greater and freer expressiveness, which sometimes ended in a blind alley of chaotic and ineffective theatricalism. The term expressionism came to the fore around 1918. The word stands for all that was not literal or representational. In its materials, the expressionist play was a curious mixture of the abstract and the concrete. It tries to present subjective values to see beyond and above reality to emotional truth. Yet it was also a drama of immediate revolt that often attacked wars of the business world or parental authority. Its construction was apt to be episodic, while the dialogue ranged from the lyric to the telegraphic. Expressionism stood behind symbols rather than scenery in its production. Bertolt Brecht, the German stalwart who started with realistic touch slipped into polemic pieces, reminiscent of expressionism in his subsequent writings. Though expressionism seems to be an ineffective gesture rather than an artistic accomplishment, some plays still covey powerful impressionist message[67].

Similar to the changes in the form of drama, stylistic character also underwent changes. Rhetoric in tone was the characteristic styles of drama for a long period in the past. Actors in those days were often robustious and periwig-pated fellows, who swayed the air with their hands and tore a passion for tatters. Eventually the drama of rhetoric gave way to drama of conversation. While the actor in the drama of rhetoric was fond of long speeches, the actor was content with brilliant lines in drama of conversation. Subsequently, drama of illusion became the reality with improvement in stage decoration. The drama of illusion, paved the way for a picture-frame proscenium, wherein the maxim action speaks louder than words became apparent. What the actor does is considered more important than what he utters[68].

The Asian Scenario

While dramatic theatres in the West were thus undergoing changes, Asian countries with their own theatrical genres were also very active in the field. Among them, the Indian tradition stands foremost for a wide variety of reasons. In the beginning, the Indian dramaturgy was superior to that of Athens by all standards (A detailed elucidation of the various stages in the evolution of the Indian drama is given in another Chapter). Suffice it to say, that theatre development in India with written plays, professional actors and playhouses ensued even before the birth of Christ.

Unfortunately, India could not maintain that lead in the succeeding centuries.

Among the other Asian countries, China and Japan had well developed theatres from the ancient past. Long before the birth of Christ, ritualistic dance and pantomime were said to have been in vogue in China. From A.D. 500 historical plays seem to have their beginning. As the theatre grew in importance, plays grew in numbers, though poor in literary quality. It is reported that one dynasty produced 280, another 690 plays[69]. Eventually, an era of expressionism ushered in with works of better quality. Most of the dramas were melodramas with happy endings. As an author adds, "the Chinese stage probably goes far beyond the Hindu in formalism, in the abstract and the symbolic"[70]. The actors used to learn and practice gestures that are as minutely symbolic as those of the Indians and Javanese. In the villages, travelling companies used to put up theatres of bamboo and matting to hold in standing position nearly one thousand spectators. The troupe might use a temple courtyard with a play related to the god of the local shrine. The performances were free, and the actors were paid by a rich native or by popular subscription. The permanent theatres in the cities were known as "tea houses" as the audience used to pay for tea, the national beverage, instead of paying for the show. The Chinese actors who are known as "Scholars of the Pear Tree", had to undergo rigorous training. Starting from childhood, they studied pantomime, hand gestures, gymnastics as well as voice. A well trained actor learned not only the lines, but also the business and make up of a hundred to two hundred roles.

In Japan, where native fertility rituals held sway, *Bugaku* and other pantomimic dances were adopted from continental countries. The performers usually in mask danced with music in a square raised stage. The dances were meant, first for the courts which patronised them and then for the priests. Out of *Bugaku* sprang up, the other distinguished forms of drama like *Noh*, *Kyogen* and *Kabuki* of Japan. It was a priest named Kanami and his son Zeami who are credited with having introduced *Noh* during sixteenth century. Staging first in the courtyard of the temple, *Noh* moved to the palace and later to the homes of aristocrats and wealthy commoners. Most of the scripts numbering two hundred and forty were written by Kanami or his son. All of them were long one act plays. Most of them "drawn from historical or religious events, both Japanese and Chinese, or present the virtues of Budhist philosophy, the sin of lust and murder, the vanity of worldly things and the blessed happiness of forgiveness in the after life"[71]. *Kyogen*, on the other hand, renders a kind of comic relief in the place of the tragic temper of *Noh*. *Kyogen* is some kind of highly humorous short play with only two or three characters. *Kabuki*, the third model, is reported to have been created by O. Kni, a priestess who lived around 1600. *Kabuki* means song, dance and action or play. Between acts or plays, there may be dances, pantomimes with narrative and music dramatic dialogue without dance or music or a combination of all the three dramatic elements. As in China, the training starts from childhood. Most of the theatres is now in a debased condition and consequently, all the three classical forms of drama have to struggle for survival[72].

Notwithstanding the promising start, the subsequent development of dramatic theatres in Asia has not been on healthy lines. Instead, they exhibited signs of stagnation and decay in course of time. The theatrical tradition of India and China had perpetuated, as Hegel noted, "a natural vegetative existence even to the present time"[73].

Conclusion

The foregoing survey sheds light on the significant role of economic factors in the development of drama from its inception. During the Greek period, drama could flourish and entertain all the citizens because slave labour provided the necessary material input. The same is the case during the Roman period. The Church and its institutions provided the material base during the years following the fall of ancient Rome. Towards the end of the Middle Ages, the kings and nobles stepped into the field as patrons of drama. Though the kings and nobles provided the means to the artists to engage in dramatic activities, they retained the services of the artists for their own entertainment. Instances are numerous, where the so called patrons propped up drama for the purpose of maintaining their reputation. The entertainment needs of the ordinary people, especially in the countryside, were met by the bards who toured with their rustic but very often vulgar performances. Since the Middle Ages, actors and dramatists became regular recipient of monetary remuneration. Actors on their part, also toured in different parts of the country by forming troupes of their own. However, from the sixteenth century onwards business men also stepped in the field ostensibly for making a gain. In most of the countries, some of the artists themselves assumed the role of businessmen by organising companies of their own and pursued dramatic activities under the banner of such companies. The actors and other artists, in turn could become the beneficiaries of such developments by appropriating an income in proportion to their calibre. When it became a business venture, the recoupment of the cost from the audiences who paid an entrance fee for seeing the performance became a fiat accompli. Apparently, it was the audience' patronage which sustained dramatic theatres during the modern period. How the audience patronage has been hijacked by the technologically mediated drama would be explored in the next chapters.

NOTES AND REFERENCES

1. Hamilton Clayton (2004); *The Theory of Theatre and other Principles of Dramatic Criticism* (Online Reader, Project Gutenburg) p. 1.
2. Cherry Sheldon (1958); *The Three Thousand Years Drama Acting and Stage Craft* (Longman Green & Co.) p. 36.
3. Hamilton, Clayton (2004); *op. cit.*, p. 44.
4. Esslin, Martin (1987); *How the Signs of Drama Create Meaning on Stage and Screen* (New York, Metheun) p. 28.
5. Hamilton Clayton (2004); *op. cit.*, p. 14.
6. *The Poetics of Aristotle* translated by S.H. Butcher (An Electronoic Classic Series Publication Pennsylvania University) p. 10.
7. The Poetics of Aristotle; *op. cit.*, p. 7.
8. Baldry Harold. C. (1979); "Theatre and Society in Greek and Roman Antiquity" in Redmond James (ed.); *Drama and Society* (Cambridge University, Press) p. 11.
9. Macgowan Kenneth and Melnitz William (1955); *The Living Stage: A History of World Theatre* (*Englewoods, Cliffs, Prentice Hall*) p. 26.
10. The budget for the festival was estimated by Mitchell at not less than 40 talents per year (about 3/4million dollars) see Baumol. William J. (1971); "Economics of Athenian Drama: Its Relevance for the Arts in a Small City Today" in *The Quarterly Journal of Economics, Vol.* lxxxv August 1971, No. 3 reprinted in Ruth Towse (ed.) (1997) *Baumol's Cost Disease* (Cheltenham, Edgar Elgar) p. 374.
11. Baumol William. J. (1971) in Ruth Towse; *op. cit.*, p. 373.
12. Macgowan and Melnitz (1955); *The Living Stage: A History of World Theatre.* (Eglewoods Cliffs, Prentice Hall), p. 32.
13. Baumol William. J. (1971); *in Ruth Tows; op. cit.*, p. 366.
14. Macgowan and Melnitz (1955); *op. cit.*, p. 27.
15. Macgowan and Melnitz (1955); *op. cit.*, p. 28.
16. Macgowan and Melnitz (1955); *op. cit.*, p. 50.
17. Macgowan and Melnitz (1955); *op. cit.;* p. 54.
18. Macgowan and Melnitz (1955); *op. cit.;* pp. 55-62.
19. Alice B. Fort and Kates Herbert. S. (1935); "Drama of the Middle Ages" in *Minute History of Drama* (New York Grosset & Dunlop); p. 7.

20. Macgowan and Melnitz (1955); *op. cit.*; p. 62.
21. Koningson Elsie (1979); "Religious Drama and urban society in France at the end of Middle Ages" in Remond James (ed.); *Drama and Society* (Cambridge University Press) p. 29.
22. Macgowan and Melnitz (1955); *op. cit.*, p. 5.2.
23. Macgowan and Melnitz (1955); *op. cit.*, p. 53.
24. Macgowan and Melnitz (1955); *op. cit.*, p. 83.
25. Macgowan ad melnitz (1955); *op. cit.*, p. 100.
26. Macgowan and Melnitz (1955); *op. cit.*, p. 110.
27. Real the Spanish coin of 16th century was stated to be equivalent to 12.5 Cents; *see also* Macgowan and Melnitz (1955); *op. cit.*, p. 127.
28. Macgowan and Melnitz (1955); *op. cit.*, p. 134.
29. Macgowan and Melnitz (1955); *op. cit.*, see pp. 141-45.
30. Macgowan and Melnitz (1955); *op. cit.*, p. 147.
31. Macgowan and Melnitz (1955); *op. cit.*, p. 145.
32. Hamilton Clayton (2004); *op. cit.*, p. 14.
33. Hamilton Clayton (2004); *op. cit.*, p. 23.
34. Prakash Anand (2013); *Critical Interpretation of English Drama* (New Deli, Wisdom Press) p. 37.
35. Macgowan and Melnitz (1955); *op. cit.*, p. 181.
36. Williams Gary Jay (2010); *Theatre History: An Introduction* (London, Routledge Taylor and Francis Group), p. 178.
37. Oates Mary. I and Baumol William. J. (1972); "On The Economics of the Theater in Renaissance London" in *Swedish Journal of Economics 1972* Reproduced in Ruth Towes; *op. cit.*, p. 386.
38. Macgowan and Melnitz (1955); *op. cit.*, p. 179.
39. Williams Gary Jay (2010); *op. cit.*, p. 175.
40. Oates Mary. I and Baumol William (1972); "On the Economics of the Theater in Renaissance London" in *Swedish Journal of Economics 1972* reproduced in Ruth Towse (ed.); *op. cit.*,. p. 387.
41. *Ibid.*; p. 380.
42. www//historyworldnet/world works/in
43. Oates Mary I-and Baumol William. J. (1972); "On the Economics of the Theater in Renaissance London, Reproduced in Ruth Towse (ed.); *op. cit.*, p. 397.
44. Magowan and Melnitz (1955); *op. cit.*, p. 150.
45. Macgowan and Melnitz (1955); *op. cit.*, p. 189.
46. 20 sous the French coin of 16th century was equilant to two shillings and two pence of Great Britain see also Macgowan and Melnitz (1955); *op. cit.*, p. 214.
47. Macgowan and Melnitz (1955); *op. cit.*, p. 217.
48. Macgowan and Melnitz (1955); *op. cit.*, p. 221.
49. Macgowan and Melnitz (1955); *op. cit.*, p. 222.
50. Macgowan and Melnitz (1955); *op. cit.*, pp. 230-31.
51. Macgowan and Melnitz (1955); *op. cit.*, p. 253.

52. Macgowan and Melnitz (1955); *op. cit.*, 259.
53. Quoted by M acgowan and Meltniz (1955); *op. cit., see* p. 327.
54. Macgowan and Meltniz (1955); *op cit.*; p. 326.
55. Macgowan and M Elnitz (1955); *op. cit.*, pp. 411-21.
56. Macgowan and Melnitz; *op. cit.*, p. 412.
57. Quoted by Macgowan and Melnitz (1955); *op. cit., see* pp. 413-14.
58. Macgowan and Melnitz (1955); *op. cit.*, p. 285.
59. Macgowan and Melnitz (1955); *op. cit.*, p. 289.
60. Macgowan and Melnitz (1955); *op. cit.*, p. 291.
61. Magowan and Melnitz (1955); *op. cit.*, p. 371.
62. Macgowan and Melnitz (1955); *op. cit.*, p. 373.
63. Macgowan and Melnitz (1955); *op. cit.*, p. 383.
64. *www//brauch.cuny.edu/library alumini/online*
65. Macgowan and Melnitz (1955); *op. cit.*, p. 435.
66. Macgowan and Melnitz (1955); *op. cit.*, see pp. 437-42.
67. Macgowan and Melnitz (1955); *op. cit.*, p. 458.
68. *Hamilton Clayton* (*1955*); *op. cit.*, p. 26.
69. Macgowan and *Melnitz* (1955); *op. cit.*, p. 302.
70. Macgowan and Melnitz (1955); *op. cit.;* p. 304.
71. Macgowan and Melnitz (1955); *op. cit.*, p. 312.
72. Macgowan and Melnitz (1955); *op. cit.*, p. 323.
73. Tilli Steve (2012); The "The Case Against World Theatre History" in *Theatre Quartely*, Vol. XXVII Nov. 2012.

3

Entry of Technologically Mediated Drama of Culture Industry

While theatrical performances were undergoing changes in the themes and style of the plays and in the very shape of stage, a new development was in the offing. It was the entry of the technologically mediated drama like cinema and tele-serial, by which culture industry became a key player in the realm of art and cuture. As already mentioned earlier in the Introduction, culture industry denotes the production of culture on factory lines for the purpose of making a gain by selling the product in the market. Drama, one of the earliest and foremost cultural activity, relies heavily on material inputs. In turn, as years rolled by, drama became more of a regular economic activity organised on commercial lines particularly since the Elizabethan period. Eventually, the technologically mediated drama of the culture industry emerged in the scene towards the close of the nineteenth century as an aftermath of the ongoing process of technological advancement.

How it transformed itself from that of an artistic activity to that of a product of culture industry, what are the further developments of the technologically mediated drama as an integral part of culture industry, the differences between drama and technologically mediated drama and the implications of such developments on live drama and on culture and society are issues requiring serious investigation. As an artistic activity, drama is concerned with the representation of human activities on a stage, on the basis of a predetermined narrative. Actors come to the stage and perform the role of the character assigned to them by imitating, as if the actor is the same character invariably with the help of various other inputs. Technology per se, does not enter in the picture on a significant scale. With the invention of electricity, drama also started to use technology on a limited scale by introducing sound and light in the theatre. However, the spectacular advancement in technology has paved the way for the emergence of technologically mediated drama of culture industry. It was not a sudden transformation of drama as technologically mediated drama, but the gradual evolution over a period of time. If so, how such an evolution had its beginnings which culminated in the emergence of technologically mediated drama?

Beginnings of Motion Pictures

Motion pictures and tele-serials, are the outcome of the efforts of many scientists and researchers stretching back to many years. They have emerged as the cumulative result of different inventions in the field of technology and innovations in business and artistic fields. Accordingly, certain authorities maintain that there is some sort of fusion of technology, art and economics in the very origin of motion pictures. As they add, "Out of the technological mechanism of projecting motion pictures invented by Edison, and persons like Marey, Lumiere brothers, Green Paul and Skladanowsky, the efforts of showmen, or rather producers, like Melies, Porter, and Griffith created an art. The commercial success of the shows, in the music halls and variety halls in Europe, where these moving pictures were exhibited for their premier show, led to the spread of cinema throughout Europe and America through the agency of "fairground showmen"[1].

It was Thomas Alva Edison who started the ball rolling in 1887 by projecting his Kinetoscope to a paying audience. The device was a crude projector suitable for viewing moving pictures by looking through a slit in the top of a box. Prior to that he, with the help of his assistant Dickson, had invented Kinetograph, the first film camera, capable of taking photographs of moving pictures. These inventions were rendered possible as a result of a series of inventions made earlier by a host of scientists and technicians. Notable among them were the invention of photography, taking of negative pictures and printing positives, roll films and the celluloid film of George Eastman. The discovery of the principle of persistent vision which provided the scientific basis for exhibiting moving pictures of an event, by taking still photographs one after another in succession, became handy for presenting moving pictures and exhibiting them. Most of Edison's experiments were conducted in Black Maria, his laboratory which thus became the first film studio.

While Edison's work was suitable for seeing moving pictures by peeping through the slit of a box, the Lumiere brothers were succeeful in projecting moving pictures on a screen through an instrument, the Cinematographe, invented by them. They gave a public show of

Cinematographe, on a cold Saturday night, in December 1895, to a paying public at Salon Indien, in Paris. With that, cinema was born, though in a humble way. The most famous film shown by Lumieres on that historic moment was "La Sortie de l'Usine Lumierea Lyon (Workers living in Lumiere factory)", a fifty foot reel depicting exactly as its title announces. The early films of Lumieres as with that of most early films were known as actualities which simply depict regular everyday events as they unfold. By 1903, the Lumieres had created over two thousand experimental films which they hurriedly exhibited in many parts of the world including Mumbai in India. People flocked in all those places where they screened their actualities, the marvel of the century[2].

In those days when film industry had its birth pangs, a clamour for entertainment was strong from the growing working class who congregated in the burgeoning industrial centres. They had not only enough money, but also leisure time. However, there was no avenue to utilise their leisure time. The few dramatic theatres which were then operating in the urban centres were insufficient to meet the growing demand for entertainment. The exhibition of moving pictures had its beginnings at such a critical period when there was a real vacuum in the entertainment field. Not surprisingly, people thronged in large numbers in the parlours, and other centres, where those scientific curiosities as they were then looked upon, were exhibited by the pioneering inventors. Edison opened his coin operated kinetoscope parlour in New York and other public places. Spectators paid anywhere from five to twenty-five cents to peep through the shows of snippets that ranged from music halls, comic sketches, historical reconstructions and the most popular footage, the boxing matches[3]. Lumieres, on the other hand travelled around the world and showed the pictures in the theatres. Seeing the demand for such exhibitions, fairground showmen came forward and carried on the business, in every nook and corner. In close succession to the sensational demand for the shows, Harry Davis, an innovative businessman, opened a five cent theatre of his in Pittsburg, a large industrial centre with remarkable degree of success. Within three years of its opening over 10000 such theatres, labelled Nickelodeons came into existence in USA. Another imaginative commercial enterprise was the famous Hale's theatre. George Hale, an ex- fireman, opened his shows in a railway coach type theatre, in which spectators had the sensation of sitting in a railway coach, while seeing the shows. In England, a cheaper type of entertainment halls known as penni-gaff sprang up. On the heels of those successful ventures, permanent cinemas with seating capacity were in the offing. Ticket charges varied from one dollar to one dollar and a half for the first run cinemas to five cents for the sixth run in the suburban cine- theatres in the US.

Originally showmen used to purchase films from the producers and exhibit them. With the growth of cinema halls, hiring of films for exhibition, as it is done today, came into existence. Instead of seeing the same film again and again, demand for new films at regular intervals became strong. In response to it, exhibitors who could not purchase films frequently, started to hire films to meet the demands of the audience. Thus, film exchanges began to grow up with hiring of films on a sliding scale of charges, according to the age of the copy and exclusivity of the hire. Thus distribution of films became another development in the growth of film industry.

Edison, the pioneering producer did not fail to take patent for his business. Subsequently in 1908, he in collaboration with others formed Motion Picture Patents Company (MPPA) for retaining their monopoly in the field. In order to escape from the monopoly hold of MPPA, certain independent producers who were interested in motion picture business moved to Hollywood, then an unknown jungly place in the south western corner of the US. In France, Charles Pathe formed his own monopoly concern. In course of time, other businessmen with capital entered in the fray, and film became a monopoly of those businessmen. The earlier businessmen who entered in the film business world were labelled as fur dealers and cloth spongers. Nevertheless, cinema slipped permanently into the hands of regular businessmen with money. On this change, E.W. and M.M. Robson prophetically observed that "they were no more aware that they were advancing a social process, than were the merchant princes of the fifteenth century aware that they were laying the foundation of nineteenth and twentieth century capitalism"[4].

The earlier films, which amused people, were brief snippets lasting 15 seconds to one minute. They were shot in Edison's studio. They featured mainly vaudeville performers performing their various stage acts, such as Little Egypt's belly dancing or Sandow the Strong man posing, natural scenes or replica of some spectacular event which lasted for one or two minutes[5]. The showmen and other producers were not sure as to how long the glamour would last. Interestingly, when Melies, a pioneering film artist, approached Lumieres with the idea of purchasing Cinematographe, the latter discouraged him by saying that it could be a scientific curiosity and beyond that, it has no commercial future. However, the artistic element, which were built into it, subsequently sustained it as a growing economic venture. The man who opened the new path in film was Melies. Himself a magician by training, he, by his spectacle films, displayed how to make narrative films by means of artificially arranged scenes. Taking the cue from him, Edwin Porter with his *Great Train Robbery,* released in 1903, introduced the idea of narrating a story through the medium of moving pictures. The production of this film started a gold rush fever which has had no equal since then[6]. During the next few years David Wark Griffith, laid the foundation of cinematic art which was to remain unchanged in the years to come. With his masterpiece "*The Birth of a Nation*", motion picture "was studying screen grammar and pictorial arithmetic"[7]. In the words of an authority, "Griffith advanced not only the notions of narrative brought forth by directors such as Porter but used and progressed camera techniques and the art of cinematography"[8]. Till then cinema-goers saw a succession of many different films each between one and fifteen minutes of varying genres such as carton newsreels, comedies, travelogues, sport films and gymnastic pictures. After the mid 1910s, going to the cinema meant watching a feature film of two to three hours, based on a dramatic theme of a famous story[9]. Thus, with motion picture, a mutated form drama was born.

One of the significant developments in the evolution of cinema is the rise of star system. During the initial days, the stars remained anonymous. They were employees of the companies which held out against identifying their artists for economic reasons, although the audience wanted to know about them. Eventually by 1910, the star system started to appear in America and within a few years it shot up into disproportionate importance. Inevitably, stars became the main source of attraction to the film-goers. Some of the stars could command as high as $10000 in a week for their services. Other countries like Italy and Russia had stars from the very beginning, though not so prominent as in the US[10].

Further developments in technology had its impact on cinema. The most important among them was sound. With sound the stature of the industry went very high. Till then, the large cinemas supplemented the feature with orchestra, vaudeville, or some other kind of live musical entertainment. After the invention of talkies, the system of hiring supporting entertainments disappeared from the film world. There was thus a definite improvement in the quality. As Turner pointed out, "the reproduction of dialogue reconnected the feature film with real life and the industry rapidly developed a system of conventions for shooting and cutting dialogue"[11]. Cultural specific films also became a reality with sound. Another development was the production of colour films which boosted the appeal of the industry still further. However, film making moved permanently, towards commercial lines with an industrial organisational structure in which the production system corresponding to the manufacturing, the distribution system to the wholesaling and the exhibition of the movies in cinema halls, to the retailing became the regular components. Nevertheless, original works of art of enduring quality also came out of films occasionally. As Jowett and Linton aptly put, "the movies have a longer and more glamorous history than most other forms of mass mediated culture, and more of an aura of art about them in spite of the fact that creating art is not the major objective of movie-making"[12].

Origin of Television

What transpires in cinema is the exhibition of prints of moving plays in theatres scattered in different localities at a fixed time on a day. They cannot be exhibited anywhere and everywhere without taking the actual copies or the print. In those cases of very successful pictures more copies are being taken for exhibition in more localities. Time and space delimit the exhibition of motion pictures. On the other hand, television, another novel technological invention, facilitates the relay at will in any locality by telecasting it.

Television had a humble beginning culminating from the experimentations and inventions by a host of technicians, engineers and scientists from different parts of the world as in that of cinema. If so, how it emerged as an epoch making technological invention?As in the case of many other inventions of the modern period, a number of persons have contributed their share to the development of television. Among them Paul Nipkov, John Logie Baird, Vlamider K.Zworykin, David Sarnoff and Phillo Fransworth, stand foremost. Experimentation, on the development of television had its simultaneous origin in different parts of the world during the closing decades of nineteenth century. Most of them were mere experimentations till the outbreak of the First World War. Credit should go to Paul Nipkov, a German for having invented in 1884, a mechanical device for transmitting pictures through the scanning disc. Images could be transmitted through the scanning disc by using a series of wires between the disc and the receiver. Pictures were scanned by punctuating holes in the disc and rotating the disc by which spectators could get the impression of a continuation of events as per the principle of persistent vision. Nipkov's device was a crude one which lacked many components to relay the clear picture of an activity or event. However, his invention became a handy instrument which could be used for further experimentation by other scientists. Quite interestingly, Philo Farnsworth, took the cue from Nipkov's device and started experimentation on transmission of pictures in 1921, when he was only a fifteen year old school boy. He pursued his efforts in collaboration with some of his friends and by 1930, he could perfect some form of television system. Around this time, Zworykin, a Russian immigrant, who had made some experiments before the Revolution, was also in the field for developing electronic television system. He could succeed in inventing iconoscope, a kind of television pick up tube, which was perfected by 1930, after making further experimentation. He entered into a patent dispute with Farnsworth, which was adjudged in favour of the latter. However, Fransworth collaborated with Zworykin by becoming a licensed partner of the Radio Corporation of America (RCA), in which Zworykin was employed. RCA, with the two pioneers in its roll, in turn, could complete the TV system by 1936. However, the actual broadcasting was delayed on account of certain patent disputes and licensing formalities.

While experimentations and inventions were thus going on in the USA, Great Britain was not far behind. The leading light in Great Britain was John Logie Baird, who led the path culminating in the invention of television. By 1932, British Broadcasting Corporation (BBC) made a working arrangement with him, by which he was ensured financial support to pursue the experimentation. Though he made a breakthrough in the matter, BBC made a parallel agreement with EMI company which was linked with RCA of USA for the development of TV. Eventually, BBC terminated the agreement with Baird and BBC succeeded in broadcasting TV with the support of EMI on 2nd Nov 1936. The presence of Chinese jugglers, American dancers, newsreels and speeches, and especially composed song "Television" sung by Adle Dixon, were some of the charming elements, which graced the occasion. Surprisingly, Britain could thus march ahead of the US in the race for public transmission of TV programmes[13]. Nevertheless, the experimentation with TV was in full swing in the US and on April 1938, TV was formally inaugurated there by Roosevelt, the US President himself. Throughout the period of experimentation, France and Germany were not idle and they could also succeed in developing television system in their own soil.

The outbreak of the Second World War compelled the stakeholders to suspend the works relating to television. Once the war was over, there was a flurry of activities leading to further developments in television. By 1948, as many as 109 TV stations were sanctioned in the US with a coverage of nearly 87 million people. Another important development was the introduction of colour TV. By this, it could become more natural and attractive. With the invention of video tape, a new instrument, programmes could be recorded or replayed or relayed. Continuity of programmes and location shooting could also be made easily with the video. The introduction of cable system was another important development. When television was introduced it was difficult to get the pictures relayed in far way places, even with the help of powerful antenne. Very often, the signals were obstructed by the mountains and tall buildings. As a way out, Cable connections were made to houses in the low lying areas. Cables located in the hill tops were suitable to pick up signals from different stations and transmit them to the households through cable hook up. The transnational hook up with ability to carry signals to the receiving sets in far off places was another development. With the invention of satellite linking system, programmes from anywhere in the world can be retransmitted with the cable system. In turn, consumers get the benefit of connecting their TV set with as many as 100 stations by linking with cables. TV has in other words, emerged as an international or transnational phenomenon, defying national boundaries[14]. Side by side, there was a spurt in the sale of TV sets and watching TV programmes became a habit with more number of people in all parts of the world.

Though television was a scientific invention accomplished by scientists, the support of business men with financial resources was very crucial for the experimentations leading to its invention. In fact, it was Sarnoff, the business manager of RCA, who brought Philo Fransworth into a collaborative agreement with Zworykin after paying $1 million as reward. Though Edison was a scientist, he pursued his enterprises on business lines. The people who moved to Hollywood to escape from the grip of Edison were pure businessmen. Huge amount of money was required for setting up TV stations. Inevitably, people with money alone could organise the TV system. At the same time, the potentiality of making huge profit through TV became apparent. Needless to say, there was a clamour for starting TV stations. Eventually, development of TV slipped permanently into the hands of entrepreneurs with big capital resources at their disposal. In the US, big corporate companies emerged at the scene and competed with each other for monopolising TV business. Thus three monopoly networks, the NBC, CBS and ABC, shared the TV business among themselves by dividing the vast majority of TV stations. Most of the broadcasting stations were converted as affiliates to these big corporate bodies. On the other hand, in Great Britain, the development of TV has been for a long time under the state with the BBC, exercising the authority on behalf of the state. In India also, television was a state monopoly for long. Since 1990s, private channels are allowed to operate and as on today as many as 900 channels operate here.

As in the case of films, short programmes were relayed during the early stages of TV. Most of them consisted of sport events, like football match, baseball, tennis, boxing, news, studio production of plays, musical shows and old movies. Television followed the foot steps of radio and film industry before emerging as a full-fledged industry. In fact, during the initial days television play remained a broadcast of stage theatre without the use of any television technique. However, with further advancement in technology, a new style in format emerged. In the words of Mitra, "as technique improved, the notions of visual space and light re-examined and plays were transformed into tele-plays where multiple cameras shot/reverse shot eye-line, catching a variety of other textual strategies were used to develop the tele-play, as a well developed set of programmes"[15]. Inevitably, many members of the crew and themes from radio and movie moved to TV. The ascendancy of television marked a fall in the attendance in cinemas. Naturally, there was a tug of war between TV and cinema. Gradually there was a thaw in the cold war between the two which eventually resulted in mutual cooperation. In the US, for instance, well over 100 series on American television were using cinematic genres of detective, spy, and war spy, and war stories. TV made experiment with almost all forms of programmes with an eye on capturing the attention of the audience. Eventually, entertainment programmes acquired prominence and most of the television formats and templates were evolved around entertainment.

Television is a technological device through which messages, events, performances, etc., can be telecast far and wide. The audiences, or the spectators, receive the contents of what is telecast with the help of receiving set. TV stations known as TV studios on their turn, prepare different kinds of programmes and relay them practically almost all the twenty-four hours of the day. The most important among them are news, documentaries, quiz, melodrama, detective stories, sports, films and tele -serials. They are potentially suitable to inform, instruct, or entertain the audience who watch them. Of the different kinds of programmes, those meant for entertainment have become the most important. Even informational programmes are presented with the necessary ingredients suitable for entertainment. Among the entertainment programmes, tele-serials, otherwise known as soap operas stand as the most important.

Once television, the marvel of the century was invented by the scientists and technicians, businessmen as mentioned earlier took the reins of TV and converted it into an industrial concern as in the case of cinema.

The products, which television produces do not fall within the category of tangible commodities proper, but within the category of service products which meet the mental or spiritual rather than material needs of man. At the same time, television per se, is only a technological instrument through which ideas and information can be communicated to an audience located in different places. Television stations on their part, prepare programmes and transmit them to the audience sitting in their homes at far off places. Preparation of programmes and transmission involve high cost. Cost goes up high, if the programmes are dramatic performances, requiring the services of actors and other material inputs, etc. Apparently, the problem posed is, how to cover the cost and make a profit? One sensible method is to charge a fee from the people who owns a TV set. It was the method adopted in Great Britain and in India for a long period of time. But can it be sufficient to make a gain posed as a problem to the people who ventured in the TV business. As a way out, the business minded Americans introduced an ingenuous method by which they could not only recover the full cost but also make a gain. The modus operandi runs on the following lines. Being a communication instrument, advertisements can be transmitted very effectively through TV. At the same time, TV can serve as a very useful media suitable for producing different forms of artistic products. Taking advantage of those possibilities, advertisers also entered in the fray for the purpose of advertising their products in the market through television. Mere advertisement may not be effective. They therefore devised an ingenous method by which pieces of advertisements are inserted in the middle of interesting artistic products like films and other dramatic performances. Tele-serials and motion pictures form the highly attractive entertainment programmes of television, though other programmes like news, sports events, and information programmes are also produced or created by television and transmitted for the consumption needs of the audiences. They are induced to watch programmes by offering them as a free service or at minimum price. The programmes are made on factory lines in such a way as to attract the maximum number of audience. Thus the television is converted as a regular industry, i.e., the culture industry, which supplies its products at low price to the audience through the connivance of the advertisers. The channels in turn, cover the cost of programmes through a dual pricing system by which they sell the air time to the sponsors or charge a fee on advertisements inserted in the middle of the programmes. They charge differential rates with higher rates during prime time when audience attendance is pretty high.

The position of the advertisers who meet the cost of programmes is somewhat similar to that of the kings and nobles of the Middle Ages who patronised cultural activities during those days. The patrons paid for the drama or other forms of art, not for the sake of art as such, nor as a charitable work. Instead, the purpose was invariably for meeting their own cultural and entertainment needs or to boost their reputation. Similarly, the advertisers sponsor the programmes in the TV for promoting the sale of their goods. They offer the programmes free of cost to the audience with the expectation of an increased sale of their own products. As the adage goes, he who pays the piper sets the tune. Similarly, advertisers determine the content and its style in such a way as to attract more number of audience. The channels operate as some sort of middlemen who deliver the audience to the advertisers. However, the channels fix the charge for the programmes on the basis of the ratings of the programmes.

Among the dramatic formats of TV, mini-serial or soap opera stands as the foremost. It is a serial format inherited from radio with liberal incorporation of cinematic format mingled with theatrical tradition. The name soap opera has originated as soap companies like Protector, and Gamble promoted the genre. Soap operas became very popular in South America where they are known as telenovela. It is appealing to the rich and the poor alike and the central theme revolves around the moral that wealth cannot bring happiness. In the opinion of Baker, soaps are specific genres of television, not only in their narrative form but also in their pivotal themes which centre on the sphere of interpersonal relationships. The storyline with most of the serials are loosely parallel revolving around marriage and family, though some of them contain attempts to shock the audience with rapes, extra marital affairs, conspiracies, kidnapping and even murders. Normally, it runs for months with each episode lasting for about 30 minutes duration. As Joseph quotes from an author, the paradigmatic structure of soaps itself, is the presentation of never ending narratives with each episode presenting an unanswered question[16]. They are staged in the home surroundings with each episode designed in such a way as to hook the audience to the next one.

The programmes, particularly relating to the dramatic performances like serials are produced in such a way as to attract more number of audiences. The quality of the programmes in terms of artistic point may not therefore be very high. As Jowett enjoins, "creating an art is not the major objective of movie making"[17]. Not surprisingly, Federal Communications Commission (FCC) has derisively described television as "the literature of the illiterate, the culture of the low brow, the wealth of the poor, the privilege of the underprivileged and the executive club of the excluded masses"[18]. Since it meets the entertainment needs of the ordinary working class, it nurtures what is known as mass culture for attracting the masses.

Differences between Theatrical Drama and Technologically Mediated Drama

While drama forms one of the oldest cultural activity, technologically mediated drama is the product of an industry –the culture industry, evolved only recently. In the words of Karnard, "what is common to all of them is drama-I mean human beings pretending to be some one else, and acting out a story, which is of interest to the viewers"[19]. However, as Mathur states, film is a "manufactured cultural presentation" and "drama is a creative stage production"[20]. Drama per se, reflects life in its full reality[21]. It creates "reality by using real human beings and often also real objects to create its fictional universe"[22]. In the mediated drama all those elements except the histrionic skill of the human beings are created by technology on commercial lines for making gains. Accordingly, it was treated as a business activity as early as in 1915 by the courts in the US which held "the moving picture is a business pure and simple originated and conducted for profit"[23]. In so doing, it became a branch of culture industry. Apparently, there can be a wide range of differences between the two.

Before proceeding to explore this issue, a word of explanation on the locus of mediated drama as branch of culture industry would not be wide off the mark. According to Steinert, a wide variety of activities fall within the ambit of culture industry, or it relates to a wide variety of activities including mediated drama. Though he has not clearly demarcated the borderline of culture industry, he has by implication includeded newspaper and paperbacks, radio and records, art prints and film, television and video, and finally multi-media, PCS and the net as the important components of culture industry[24]. Throsby, an authority on the economics of culture, has introduced a model with the locus of origin of creative ideas as the centre of culture industry with more and other inputs combining to produce a wider range of products[25]. On the basis of his model, music, drama, dance, theatre, literature, the visual arts such as video art, computer and multi-media art and so on, form the core of the industry. Those industries whose output qualifies as a cultural commodity but with lower proportion of cultural content like book and magazine, television and radio, newspaper and film form the second category. In his words, both cultural and non-cultural services are produced side by side. Though he labels many activities under the rubric of cultural activities, television and films do not find a place within the core sector. On the other hand, drama and theatre fall within the core area of culture industry. However, drama per se, is a pure cultural activity which is not staged on factory lines, though commercial considerations also assume importance with many of them. As per the norms accepted by us, those activities produced on factory lines for making a gain alone fall within the ambit of culture industry. Hesmondhalgh, another authority, includes film and television within the core area of culture industries[26]. His approach seems to be objective in the case of films and television. Similarly, Unesco's Institute of Statistics, includes "printed matter, and literature, music, visual art, cinema, and photography, radio and television games and sporting goods" within the class of culture industry[27]. Caves another authority uses the term creative industry to denote those activities coming within the purview of culture industry. In his opinion, "books and magazines publishing, the visual arts, (painting and culture), the performing arts, (theatre, opera, concerts, dance), sound recording, cinema and TV films and even fashion and toys and games" form the units of creative industries[28].

Though all of them treat drama and theatre within the rubric of culture industry, they are essentially cultural activities per se, without the involvement of technology. Apparently, they cannot be treated as industrial products, let alone as products of culture industry. However, both film and television are products which depend heavily on technology for their creation. In the case of television programmes, tele-serial or soap alone falls within the category of mediated dramatic performances enacted with the help of technology and not other programmes. (Nevertheless, television also telecasts motion pictures.) Accordingly, other activities of television do not form part of dramatic activity. Technology has also been instrumental in creating internet and video, through which mediated drama can be telecast or communicated, but they cannot form part of drama per se. Apparently, only dramatic performances in the form of motion pictures or films and tele-serials alone form technologically mediated drama proper of culture industry for the purpose of the study.

Drama presented in live form to the audience constitutes the distinguishing characteristic of theatrical drama. On the other hand, only a duplicate, or copy, of the original is exhibited to the audience in the case of the mediated drama. Since drama is presented to an audience, some sort of interaction with the audience is inherent in it. In fact, in the past, interaction with the audience was a regular phenomenon during the staging of a drama. Any mistake, or shortcoming, can not be rectified in the case of a drama. All shortcomings have to be rectified during the time of rehearsal itself. On the other hand, mediated drama is presented, or exhibited, after rectifying the mistakes at the time of acting or editing. By and large, mediated drama relies on mechanical reproduction. Mediated drama lacks the aura of originality as copies, or prints, only are exhibited or telecast. Mechanical reproduction has, in fact undermined the importance of originality in different forms of art. Furthermore, reproduction undermines the aesthetic experience bestowed by art as one of its primary concerns. As Kuspit pointed out, "reproducton levels its sensuality and with that its emotional effect, thus subverting its vitalising evocative power, and makes it seem less intelligent and subtle than it is – and that first hand experience of it can discover it to be-and with that de-aestheticizes it, that is, renders it useless as a means to the end of aesthetic experience"[29]. If it were to be so, the very question of genuine works of art coming out of mediated drama becomes somewhat meaningless.

Ordinary drama is addressed to a limited number of audience presented in a theatre. Fresh staging would be required, to cater to a new band of audience in another place or on another occasion. Motion pictures, or tele-serials, are addressed to an audience scattered in different places. They can be exhibited, or relayed, to a new band of audience on another day or place at practically nil cost of production. Furthermore, its performances are staged in different places or locations. In fact, location shooting forms an integral part in any mediated drama. Thus there is a separation of the locale of performance and locale of receiving or seeing. An illusion of non-separation is created by technology. As Mathur enjoins, "this is because of the speed and simultaneous reception of the message that the electronic media carry". Similarly, the artistic skill of the performer, the poet, the director, etc., becomes subsidiary. Close ups, reaction shots, zooms, pans, freeze shots, solarisation dissolves, etc., are the means by by which communication with the audience can be effective. In brief, as Mathur adds, "the artistry of the programme-content and performance is only a subsidiary factor"[30].

Furthermore, stage dramas fall within the category of creator oriented-works of art, while mediated dramas are basically audience oriented. Accordingly, the format is designed in such a way as to attract the audience. On the other hand, ordinary drama is a unique commodity. The same actors may not be able to display the original qualities if the drama is staged again. On the other hand, mediated drama is standardised commodity exhibited again and again on the exigencies of demand to a wider audience with practically no additional cost. Accordingly, they are meant mainly for meeting the entertainment needs of the people. Because of the focus on pure entertainment value, the mediated dramas are often looked down by scholars as artistic opiates. As an author notes, "the overwhelming tendency in film and television production, and in film and video production, as well, has been to become increasingly, sophisticated in technical terms and increasingly unsophisticated in intellectual terms. The tendency has been to rely on atmospheric locations, fluid camera movements, fast cutting, haute culture, action adventure stunts, cheap thrills and star glamour, at the expense of dialogue, characterisation, plot structure, social context or any sense of deeper meaning or purpose. Even the acting relies more on technology than on the skill of the artists. In fact dramatic performances are natural while mediated dramas are essentially artificial. The most expensive production are given the shoddiest of scripts. The most advanced technology is put in the service of storylines, and images written, produced and performed by those who have never risen to a cultural level above that of the comic strip/beer commercial mentality"[31]. The artists led by the writer maintain the upper hand in theatrical performances. On the other hand, the director gets the upper hand in technologically mediated drama. As Kirti Jain says, "TV and films are more the director's media than the actors"[32]. In fact, movie is very often regarded as the creation of the director who is otherwise known as the auteur. Not surprisingly, some authors maintain movies as the seventh form of art. Furthermore, the dramatic script is endowed with literary qualities. Even if they are not staged, they can be read and appreciated. In mediated drama, the script is relegated to an inferior position.

Ordinary drama is produced at comparatively low cost. On the other hand, mediated drama calls for high cost apparently on account of the involvement of advanced technology at different stages. Since they are produced to meet the entertainment needs of a large number of audience cost escalation becomes inevitable. Cost also shoots up on account of the high cost of cast, especially the super stars.

Impact on Drama, Economy and Culture

The origin of mediated drama is having far reaching implications on drama and culture of the society. It has adversely affected dramatic theatres. Marginalisation of drama proper is one of the serious consequences of the growth of mediated drama. The number of people attending drama has come down in all parts of the world. As Mathur notes, "of all the performing arts, it is drama, that has benefitted the least from modern mass media. In fact, one gets the impression that drama as it has grown over centuries – its blend of literature, poetry, action and expression – may perhaps in the future have no place in the media world"[33]. On the other hand, although there is a set back with the emergence of TV, large number of people still attend cinema, one component of culture industry regularly in almost all parts of the world. TV, the other component of mediated drama has emerged as an essential ingredient in the cultural life of the people. The period of time devoted for viewing TV is even more than the time devoted for work. In other words, TV has colonised practically the whole of leisure time. As Adercrombie says, "television watching occupies more time than all the other leisure pursuits combined and ranks with working and sleeping as time consuming activities,—."[34]. Dramatic performances of TV in the form of serials and other formats occupy most of the prime time programmes of TV. While stage drama faces an uncertain future with falling attendance, technologically mediated drama grows in leaps and bounds.

A corollary of the marginalisation of drama is the migration of talented actors to television and cinema. Appearance in cinema or television has become the goal of many artists, apparently on account of the glamour attached to them. In tandem to this development, the emergence of super star, as indicated earlier, is a new development with mediated drama. The system of formatting stars has emerged as a business strategy for ensuring good audience response. As already stated, products of mediated drama are created primarily for getting good return. Nevertheless, they also contain certain amount of artistic ingredients and accordingly possess their uniquiness. However, the acceptability of mediated drama by the public still remains uncertain. The presence of a superstar can neutralise this uncertainty to some extent. As Vogel writes, "it may be less risky to pay a star $1.5 million than to pay an unknown $100000; the presence of the star may easily increase the value of the property by several times that the $1.5 million salary, through increased sales in theatrical and other markets, whereas the unknown may add nothing from the standpoint of return on investment"[35]. Apparently, audiences prefer the programmes performed by such superstars who dominate the scene on account of their superior talents.

Rosen introduces another reason for the emergence of super stars. In his opinion the emergence of culture industry has reduced the real price of entertainment services, coupled with the widening of the size of the audience. At the same time, artistic remuneration amounts to a rental payment stemming from the talent of the artists. The rent-talent gradient increases with the widening of the market leading to inreased scope for each performer's audience. As he puts it, "if demand for services is sufficiently elastic – rents for sellers increase and in turn their greater concentration in the distribution of rewards among the most talented"[36]. Thus those who marshalls large size of audience get bigger size of rewards. Whatever be the rationale for the high rate of remuneration accruing to superstars, the very appearance of superstars has to be attributed to the emergence of culture industry. As Kuspit sarcastically confides, "the entertaining celebrity is a capitalist robot in a merchandising spectacle"[37].

As with the emergence of superstars, a situation in which film stars becoming the role models for a vast number of people is also on the anvil. Fans of the leading stars have been formed and they emulate the behaviour of stars in their day today life. TV stars also form high profile category, though they have not risen to the level of superstars.

One of the significant effect of the growth of culture industry is the penetration of television and cinema throughout the world. In consequence drama viewing, though of the mediated variety, has permeated throughout the world. At no time in the history of mankind humanity has exposed to drama as the present century. More drama is watched in a week or weekend than would have been watched even in a lifetime in any historical period. The growing urbanisation, the increase in disposable income, and the availability of free time are the main factors which contributed to the increase in viewership. Mention may be made in this connection, that access to cultural products was practically nil to the ordinary people in the past, when the cultural field was dominated by the so called high culture. As Gans maintains, "high culture was inaccessible to them. The social and political elite that supported high culture, not only rejected popular participation in elite activities, but made no effort to provide the rest of the society with the economic and other requirements needed to share in high culture"[38]. With the penetration of TV, even the lowest strata of society can see cultural programmes like drama easily. Television is able to penerate because it has grown as a regular household article. It finds a place invariably in the drawing room. Each person can see the programmes including drama as and when one likes it with absolute privacy. The era of the so called culture industry has witnessed not merely the scope for viewing drama for the ordinary people, but also the scope for writing dramatic works has also improved. As Esslur enjoins, "radio and television have played an important role in the rise of most vigorous period of dramatic writing in the history of British Isles since Elizabethan and Jacobean times"[39].

Among the significant developments with the emergence of mediated drama, mention may be made of the entry of economic parameters in its production and distribution in a big way. In turn, mediated drama has become an important economic activity which generates income and create employment. It is reported for instance, that media industry comprising television and films contributes nearly 0.6 per cent of the Gross Domestic Product of India and provides employment to 1.9 million jobs as on today[40]. Huge amount of money is being invested in the production of such dramas. Furthermore, spending a portion of income for seeing them has become a habit with people in almost all parts of the world. Apparently, expenditure on them has become another item in the consumer expenditure with most of the people.

On account of its appeal to a large number of people, there is a belief that movies and television are capable of influencing the behavioural pattern of people. Advertisers lavishly spend money on TV programmes apparently because of this belief. From the formative days of culture industry, such a belief was strong. A report made in 1917 by the National Council of Public Morals in Great Britain contains an interesting observation as: "moving pictures are having a profound influence upon the mental and moral outlook of millions of our young people—an influence the more subtle in that it is subconsciously exercised"[41]. Jowet tand Linton, express the view that motion picture was the first of the major mass media forms to attain the status of a massive socialising force on a national scale[42]. In the light of those views, various authors have accused mediated drama of shaping and even distorting behavioural pattern of people in society. An author maintains, "television has trivilsed and effectively destroyed the public discourse that underpins politics, education and all activities in the public sphere". He adds further that "television is transforming our culture into one vast arena for show business"[43]. Another author states that it "can lead to addiction, and withdrawal that exacerbates loneliness and overrides deeper experience of pleasure and pain"[44]. Some other authors go further and state that television and films promote sex appeal and encourage violence in society by the lavish display of sex and violence with impunity. As Williams enjoins, "it is doubtful whether before the epoch of television serials and series anything like the current proportion of dramatic attention to crime and illness had ever existed"[45]. During the course of a speech Prince of Wales came specifically on the issue and posed "do we have to tolerate an incessant menu of utterly gratuitous violence on both cinema and television-especially television, and most particularly videos"[46]. Display of such scenes in the mediated drama, can nurture a culture of violence in the society. The impact of such scenes will be very powerful with young children. Even John Major, a former British Prime Minister, had come out vehemently on the "relentless diet of violence" and its "serious effects on the young". Furthermore, TV the most important component of culture industry has been castigated by an author as "one eyed monster" which "snatches children in its maw and nurtures as some kind of monster"[47]. Abercombie who has expressed doubts about the effects of mediated drama in fostering violence in the society succinctly states thus: "it is often claimed that violence on television causes viewers or some viewers at any rate to become violent in real life. This is thought to be true of some vulnerable sections, of the audience, especially children"[48]. Apparently, the potentiality of mediated drama in creating undesirable behavioural pattern in the society is beyond doubt. They have become some kind of the opium of the elite, according to Kuspit[49].

Technologically mediated drama, especially television has grown as an integral part of the culture in almost all parts of the world. TV viewing has become a regular habit with most of the people. It is reported that an American child would have spent 20000 hours watching television against only 11,000 hours in the classroom by the time he completes his school education[50]. No other institution has been able to exert so much influence on culture within a short period of its appearance.

Conclusion

In sum, mediated drama has emerged as an important branch of culture industry. Huge sums of money are being invested in them in many parts of the world. They provide employment to a large number of people wherever they have grown. A substantial portion of income is being generated by them in many parts of the world. Furthermore, spending a portion of the disposable income by the ordinary people for seeing or watching them forms a part of the consumer expenditure. Though they are supposed to be cultural products, such goods are by and large mercantile commodities with least regard to artistic qualities. Nevertheless, they throw serious threat to dramatic theatres.

NOTES AND REFERENCES

1. Oommen M.A. and Joseph. K.V. (1991); *Economics of Indian Cinema* (New Delhi, Oxford & IBH Publishers), pp. 11-13.
2. Manley Brian (2011); *Moving Pictures: The History of Early Drama in pro quest Guides* http://www.csa.com/discovery guides-main php; p. 7.
3. Manley Brian (2011); *op. cit.*, p. 5.
4. Robson. E.W. and M.M. Robson (1947): *The Film Answerback: An Historical Appreciation of Cinema* (London, John Lane and Bodlyhead Ltd.) p. 29.
5. Manley Brian (2011); *op. cit.*, p. 5.
6. Robson. E.W. and Robson. M.M. (1947); *op. cit.*, p. 35.
7. Ramsaye Terry (1964); *A Million One Nights. A History of Motion Picture* (London, Frank & Co.) p. 508.
8. Manley Brian (2011); *op. cit.*, p. 14.
9. Bakker Gerben (2008); *The Economic History of Internatinal Film Industry* (*Economic* History (http//eh.net/encycopaedia/the economic historyof-the international-fm.industry/) p. 5.
10. Bakker Gerben (2014); *op. cit.*, p. 4.
11. Turner Graeme (2006); *Film as Social Practice IV* (London, Routledge) p. 17.
12. Jowett and Linton (1980); *Movies as Mass Communication* (London Sage Publication). p. 19.
13. Joseph. K.V. quotes from Bob Mullen (1997); *Consuming Television* (Oxford, Blackwell Publishers) see Joseph. K.V. (2010); *Economics of Culture Industry; Television in India* (Delhi, Shipra Publications) p. 34.
14. Joseph. K.V. (2010); *op. cit.*, pp. 37-39.
15. Joseph. K.V. quotes from Mitra, Anand (1993); *Television in India: A Study of Mahabharat*, see Joseph. K.V. (2010); *op. cit.*, p. 92.
16. Joseph K.V. (2010); *op. cit.* pp. 93-94.
17. Jowett and Linton (1980), *op. cit.*, p. 19.
18. Quoted by Sheehan Helena (2001); in *Television as A Medium of Drama* (Dublin, RTE 1987) p. 8.
19. Quoted by Dharwadker Aparna Bhargava (2005); in *Theatre of Independence* (New Delhi, Oxford University Press), p. 125.
20. Mathur J.C. (2009): "Encounter of the Performing Arts and Modern Mass Media" in Nandi (ed.), *Modern Indian Theatre: A Reader* (New Delhi, Oxford, University Press) p. 412.
21. Sue Thornham and Tony Purvit (2005); *Television Dramas: Theories and Identities* (Palgrave Macmillan Inc.) p. 21.
22. Esslin Martin (1987); *The Field of Drama How the Signs of Drama create Meaning on Stage and Screen* (Metheun, London New York) p. 29.
23. Jowett *et al.* (1980): *op. cit.*, p. 71.
24. Steinert Heinz (2003); *Culture Industry* translated by Sally Ann Spencer (Cambridge, Polity Press) p. 75.

25. Throsby David, (2001); *Economics and Culture* (Cambridge University Press) p. 27.
26. Hesmondhalgh, David (2000): *The Cultural Industries* (London, Sage Publications) p. 28.
27. See, Lousie C Johnson (2009); *Cultural Capitals: Revaluating the Art, Remaking Urban Space* (Surrey, Asghgate Publishing Ltd.) p. 8.
28. Caves, Richard (2000): *Creative Industries: Contracts Between Art and Commerce* (Harward University Press) p. 1.
29. http//www.percotranet./archive/19kuspit.htm (2014); Kupsit Donald "Paradoxes and prolems of the Reproduction and Comodifcation of Art in the Age of Capitalist Spectacle".
30. Mathur, J.C., (2009); *op. cit.*, p. 407.
31. Sheehan Helena, (2001); *op. cit.*, p. 7.
32. Jain Kirti (2009); "Drama on Television" in Bhatia Nandi (ed.) *op. cit.*, p. 421.
33. Mathur, J.C. (2009); *op. cit.*, p. 411.
34. Abercrombie, Nicholas (1996); *Television and Society.* (Cambridge, Polity Press) p. 3.
35. Vogel, Harold (2004); *Entertainment Industry Economics: A Guide to Financial Analysis* (Oxford University Press) p. 133.
36. Joseph, K.V. quotes from Rosen Sherwin (1986); "The theory of Super Star" in *American Economic Review* Vol. 71 No. 5 *see* Joseoph, K.V. (2010); *op. cit.*, p. 140.
37. Kuspit, Donald (2014); *"Paradoxes and Problemsof the Reproduction and Commodification of Art in the Age of the Capitalist Spectacle (http;// www.percontra.net/arcive/19kuspit.htm)/* p. 4.
38. Gans, J. Herbert (1974); *Popular Culture and High Culture: An Analysis and Evaluation of Taste* (New York, Basic Books) p. 60.
39. Esslin, Martin (1993); "Electronic Media and British Drama" in *Theodore Shank: Contemporary British Theatre*), p. 180.
40. www///indiatimes.com /NEWS –MORE-for-India/FICCI
41. Jowett and Linton (1980); *op. cit.*, p. 67.
42. Jowett and Linton (1980); *op. cit.*, p. 73.
43. See Abercrombie (1996); *op. cit.*, p. 5.
44. Helena Sheehan (2001); *op. cit.*, p. 3.
45. Williams Raymond (1975); *Television Technology and Cultural Form* (London, Routledge), p. 60.
46. Abercrombie (1996); *op. cit.*, p. 6.
47. Quoted by Joseph, K.V. (2010); from Messenger, Mary Davies (2001); *Dear BBC, Children, Televisio, Story Telling an Public Sphere* (Cambridge University Press); see Joseph, K.V. *op. cit.*, p. 173.
48. Abercrombie (1996); *op. cit.*, p. 5.
49. Kupsit Donald (2014); *op. cit.*, p. 5.
50. Mullan Bob (1997); *Consuming Television* (Oxford Backwell Publishers), p. 159.

4

Dramatic Tradition of India and Its Pattern of Development in Malayalam

In Chapter 2, we have sketched out a brief review of the evolution of drama in the West and in Chapter 3, the entry of mediated drama. How the drama originated in Athens in the fifth century B.C. spread to other parts of the world and its evolution over the years was the theme of Chapter 2. A brief account of the evolution of drama in India and the pattern of its development in Kerala are delineated in this Chapter.

While the mainstream drama of the West was moving ahead on the path thrown open by Greek tragedies, for which man's struggle provided the main theme, India could claim for having evolved a strong dramatic tradition differing in content and form from Greek tradition. Unlike the human struggle as depicted in Greek tradition, the very objective of *abhinya* according to the Sanskrit dramaturgy is "to create a feeling of bliss, or *ananda,* in the minds of the spectators by revealing various mental states of a character"[1]. Significantly, in the light of the importance of drama and theatre in Indian life that "*Natyashastra* has been given the status of the fifth veda"[2].

Furthermore, *Natyashastra*, a comprehensive treatise on dramatic theatres of Bharat Muni, the legendary dramatic theoretician of India, excels *Poetics* of Aristotle in providing graphic details on various aspects of dramaturgy. His treatise offers, as Soloman enjoins, "copious data about every conceivable theoretical and practical aspect of theatre; acting and dance, music and prosody, shapes and sizes of playhouses, organisation and management of theatre companies, costuming and make- up properties and stage decorations, theories of emotions and sentiments, types and rules for dramatic composition and even requirements for critics and audiences"[3]. Apparently, Bharat Muni, belittles Aristotle as a theoretician of dramatic art. Furthermore, by giving graphic details about the shape and size of theatre, the stage preparation, organisation and management of the theatre, the seating arrangements etc., he was sensitive to the material inputs coming to the fore in staging the drama.

However, Bharat Muni narrates the mythological origin of *natyaveda* and attributes its creation to none other than the great God Brahma himself. According to Bharat Muni, while creating *natyaveda*, Brahma himself is stated to have detailed the following in graphic terms as its functions: "in it, sometimes there is reference to duty, sometimes to games, to money, to peace; in it is found laughter, fight, lovemaking, and sometimes killing of people—it teaches duty to those who bent on duty, love to those who are ill-bred or unruly, promotes self restraint on the disciplined energy in heroic persons, enlightens men of poor intellect, it gives courage to cowards, wisdom to the learned, diversion to the kings, and firmness of mind to the persons afflicted with sorrow, composure to persons agitated in the mind"[4]. Evidently, drama occupied a very dominant position, not only in the life of of an ordinary human being, but also in the social and political arena. As another author enjoins, "there is no wise maxim, no learning, no art, or craft, no device, no action that is not found in drama"[5]. In other words, drama had an all embracing characteristic, according to the Indian tradition.

Such a lengthy statement attributed to the very creator testifies the prominence given to drama in ancient India. In no other country in the world, so much importance has been assigned to drama as in India. In the words of Jain, "theatrical activity in this country has always been regarded not merely a religious ritual or only a form of entertainment, but an important means and instrument for controlling and containing the distortions arising in the life of an individual or society, and to guide them into edifying direction"[6]. Though couched in ritual language, the Sanskrit drama was basically secular in character.

However, the performance could best be understood by the elites "who are learned, wise, skilled in the arts, and sensitive" and not by the masses[7]. Apparently, they reflect the high art of later period. The main components of the genre have been a combination of acting with music. This legacy has been well preserved even in the motion pictures of the 20th century.

Such a dramatic tradition, seems to have been flourishing between sixth century B.C. to the second century A.D. A galaxy of eminent dramatists, like Bhasa, Kalidasa, Shudraka, Vishkhadatta, Sriharha,

Bhodyana etc., contributed their share in enriching Sanskrit dramatic tradition. Their contributions are hailed as outstanding works of drama. Unfortunately, excepting *Kudiattam* of Kerala, the Sanskrit tradition has totally disappeared from the county.

Sanskrit tradition gave way to what is known as folk-theatre in course of time. With regional variations, they flourished in the rural areas only and not in the urban centres. The tone and content of the medieval theatre were religious in every aspect. The *Aukinet* of Assam, *Bhagavatamela* of Tamil Nadu, *Krishnattam* of Kerala, *Kuchipadi* of Andhra Pradesh, *Dasavatar* of of Maharastra, *Rasaleela* and *Ramaleela* of Uttar Pradesh etc., are basically *Vaishnava* religious rituals, in which the performers are regarded not as human beings, but *swooraps* or incarnation of God to be worshipped as such during performance[8]. Nevertheless, they failed to attract sufficient patronage from the influential quarters and in turn deceleration set in.

The plays prepared tend to be more or less theatrical texts or production scripts full of poetry, providing for mime, music and dance. The theatres in turn, contributed in making music widely popular among the common people. With this, the folk music and many *ragas* of classical music gained popularity among the local people. The constant exposure of music for more than thousand years had made it an integral part of the taste and sensibility of the common man to the extent that it is difficult to think of our popular performances including cinema without music[9]. In the absence of good theatrical text, the actors provided flesh and blood to the skeletons contained in the script and gave vitality and meaning. In other words, it was completely a theatre of actors. Whatever be the relevance of performance, the absence of scripts expressing independent creative value was conspicuous. Any creative dramatic work was not forthcoming during those years. Nor a single playwright emerged in any of the regional languages.

Modern Period

The advent of the British colonial administration paved for the emergence of a new dramatic tradition in the country. It was on the model of British pattern with very little characteristics of Indian tradition. The creation of a feeling of pleasure or bliss by delineating different feelings of human life, as indicated earlier, formed the main objective of drama according to the Sanskrit or medieval tradition of India. On the other hand, the focus of Western line of thinking revolves around some kind of conflict between man and God, man and nature, man and man, or between various emotions, desires, and tendencies within man himself. Reckoned as a representation of life as such, it was difficult to think of drama without a conflict. In addition, there was then, a strong feeling among the Britishers that Indian culture including drama was inferior to theirs. At the same time, the British authorities successfully carved out a new class which was eager to imitate English customs and manners including their artistic activities like drama, through their educational policy.

It was at this juncture, modern drama was introduced in India by Englishmen with the staging a few dramatic performances to meet the entertainment needs of the British soldiers stationed in Calcutta, Delhi, Mumbai, Madras, etc. Sensing the possibility of making profit, a few commercial minded Indians also entered in the theatrical business by opening theatres first in Calcutta and then in Mumbai and other places. The English educated Indians, who were eager to adopt English customs and manners came in large numbers to see such dramatic performances when staged in the newly opened theatres in Calcutta. The theatres in Bengal were set up mainly in the urban centres and not in the rural sector. Most of the plays staged there were either works of English authors or written on the English model. There was very little inclination to include either the elements of Jatra, the native traditional genre of Bengalis or Sanskrit tradition, in the new dramatic works presented in the theatre, as most of the authors were either of British origin or those associated with the British tradition. The stories composed by them were based on mythologies, folk tales, historical events or contemporary social situations. However, as Jain observes, "on the whole, with very few exceptions, the creative achievements of these plays is negligible, and they are generally little more than stageable melodramas". Furthermore, they lacked the inner contradictions of human characteror or an imaginative original structure[10]. Rabindranath Tagore was perhaps the only exception. However, most of his plays were dismissed as mere poetics or poetic drama, not suitable for staging.

Taking the cue from the success of the theatre thus opened in Bengal, enterprising businessmen composed mainly of Parsis entered the field of drama in Mumbai. Though most of the theatres in Mumbai and in other parts of western India were owned by the Parsi business community, the first commercial theatre was actually started by Vishnudas Bhave, in 1853. He, by presenting in Marathi, the first ticketed show for native audience in grand Road Theatre, became the first Indian theatre entrepreneur, soon followed by Parsi companies[11]. Eventually, theatrical activities sprang up in the interior parts of Marathi and Gujarati regions. Unlike the Bengal pattern, theatrical performances contained dance and music, apparently on account of the leanings to the Indian tradition and the influence of *Tamasha*, the indigenous Marathi dramatic genre. In fact, many top ranking classical musicians began to act in the professional dramatic companies to which the audience flocked more to hear music than to see a play[12]. In the Marathi theatre, actor playwrights were also active in the picture. However, it was the Parsis who took a leading role in the growth of theatres in Mumbai and the interior parts of Gujarat, where commercials with melodramatic stories were in the fray.

The entry of Western dramatic models were delayed in the South mainly on account of a strong and deeply entrenched tradition with fanatical adherence. Later on, Western style dramas were written in Tamil, Malayalam, Telugu, Kannada and companies performing them were established. Though most of the artists were content with very low rate of remuneration, apparently on account of their keen interest in acting, some actors could command very high rate of reuneratin. Most of the plays were more or less on the model of Parsi theatre with the stories based on mythological, historical, or social events with superficial imitations of Shakespeare and other British authors or Moliere. *Sangeethanataka* or music drama was te genre which became popular in the south. On the whole, neither their form and technique had any originality, nor their content any insight or depth.

The situation in the Hindi herartland of the interior parts of India was different from that of the other regions. English education and culture were slow to penetrate in that region. As a result, the new dramatic theatres were opened a bit late. Nevertheless, Parsi theatre companies from Mumbai, eventually made inroads in that region and started to entertain the people with commercial dramas. They were able to make maximum profit by staging melodrama in spectacular manner. Though some of the gifted artists collaborated with them, the Parsi theatres were not able to make any significant contribution to the cultural life in the Hindi speaking regions.

An equally important development in the country is the appearance of dramatic theatres around different languages in India. Theatres are opened even around languages which are not spoken by a large umber of people like Manipuri, Konkani, Dogri, Maithili, Urudu, Sindhi, etc. They seem to hold on, notwithstanding the onslaught of the mediated drama and various other difficulties since independence.

The Impact of New Media and Further Developments

The appearance of the talkie era from the thirties of 20th century had far reaching impact on dramatic theatres. As a consequence, most of the theatre companies including the owners, actors, playwrights, and technicians deserted the theatres and moved to the films creating a near vacuum in the Hindi theatre. The setback was not confined to the Hindi theatre alone. As noted by Jain, in every region of the country, theatre business has come almost to a standstill around 1940s and the companies were closed down with the actors becoming jobless[13]. However, the rise of Peoples Theatre Association of the forties of 20th century gave a relief to the theatres for a short period in many parts of the country.

Since independence, there was some kind of revival of drama. The entry of good number of people in the field with the desire to engage in creative work has changed the outlook from pure commercial intention. One significant development was the attempt to incorporate elements of Indian tradition both of the ancient and medieval periods and give a new direction to drama. The leading lights who strove to give a new direction to drama include Habib Tanvar, Sombu Mitra, Uppal Dutt, Vijaya Tendulkar, Girish Karnard, K.N. Panicker, etc. With the writings of such authors, as Jain says, "there is an attempt to understand and articulate the basic philosophical and moral questions, dilemmas or contradictions of life today, the relationship between different layers of society, between individual and society and between man and society"[14]. At the same time, the government of India and various state governments also came forward with a keen interest in the development of drama. Side by side, foreign dramatists also have been taking a keen interest to understand the Indian tradition and to assimilate some of them in their genres. The dramatists belonging to different linguistic groups also began to exhibit interest in assimilating elements from other linguistic dramatic genres in their own works. A pan Indian genre maintaining Indian identity also seems to be in the offing.

Nevertheless, theatres are facing stiff competition from the new technologically mediated drama which provides entertainment at cheap rate, throughout the length and breadth of the country. The observation that the "dwindling audience interest due to the thrust of electronic media became detrimental to the healthy growth of the theatre" made by an author on Telugu theatres, holds good with all linguistic groups also[15]. However, the tide seems to have tamed by creating a niche audience through the formation of such specialised forums like childrens'dramatic clubs, women's clubs, etc. Theatre festivals which are also often being conducted invariably with full houses also constitute an indicator of positive audience response to drama in a new environment. In Andhra Pradesh, for example, as Ngabhushana Sharma concurs, "old groups and *Padya Natakam* were revived, new ones started and new scripts of diverse kinds appeared"[16]. Similarly, the outlook in Hindi theatre as Kirti Jain states "seems positive definitely in site where much experimentation in content and form takes place"[17]. At the same time, committed theatre troupes operate in almost every major town in Hindi belt, despite the exodus of artists to the media and advertising[18].

Dramatic Theatres in Malayalam

Malayalam as a distinct language is stated to have originated from the old Dravidian language during the fifteenth century. Unlike Tamil and other Dravidian languages, Malayalam borrowed heavily from Sanskrit and moved further from the old language in a new direction. Literary works in Malayalam with an overtone of Sanskrit seemed to have appeared from that period onwards. Poetic works of Cherusseri are perhaps the earliest work in Malayalam.

Proto-Dramatic (Ritual) Performances of Kerala.

Dramatic performances of rudimentary forms seem to have been quite vogue even before the origin of Malayalam as a distinct language. Most of them were ritual performances enacted in temples. Foremost among them were *Kudiattom*, *Padayani* and *Teyyam*. Among them, *Kudiattom* constitutes "one of the oldest continuously performed theatre forms, and it may well be the oldest surviving art form of ancient world"[19]. It is believed to have originated during first century AD. It is a ritual performance staged during temple festivals. Around 17th century, *Kathakali*, the world renowned genre, was evolved. Even before the appearance of *Kathakali*, *Chavittunatakam*, a Christian dramatic genre, was on the anvil, thanks to the efforts of European missionaries. It took two more centuries for the appearance of modern forms of drama in Kerala. It was Tamils who started the ball rolling by introducing modern drama in Kerala, mainly on commercial lines. Taking the cue from the Tamils, Malayalam authors also began to write Malayalam dramas and began to stage them from the last quarter of nineteenth century.

Kudiattom

Kudiattom, an ancient form of drama, is believed to be a regional derivation of Sanskrit dramatic tradition. It is found exclusively in Kerala. It is held by some scholars that the first Sanskrit work in Malayalam was composed by Sakhibhadra during the ninth century. However, there are references to Kudiyattam in *Chilapathikaram,* a first century Tamil literary work. Its acting style comprises an 'elaborate blend of symbolic gesture, stylised physical movements and chanted dialogue and verses'. Chakkiar caste was traditionally connected with this form and hence it is also known as Chakkiar Kuthu. During the performance, Chakkiar, the male actor appears in special outfits with headgear and other make- up-materials. Nangiar, women members of the same caste, also appears in *Kudiattom.* They stage the performance in *Kuthambalam,* the theatres attached to temples in conformity to the prescriptions of *Natyasastra*. Chakkiars play their performance based on Ramayana and other epics.

A four fold convention of acting, viz, vocal, physical, psychological and decoration are well preserved in *Kudiattom*. The enactment is a prolonged process stretching over a number of nights. The style and musical modes are suited to the respective sentiments. Further, as an author says, "the elaborate make- up, along with flowery crown and various ornaments uses a colour scheme symbolising the character's basic qualities"[20]. The actors undertake vigorous training, stretching for years to preserve the techniques of physical movements. The members belonging to the community maintain the age old tradition, notwithstanding the changes, in various cultural genres. Ammannur Madhava Chakkiar, Painkulam Raachakkiar, Moozhikulam Kochukuttan Chakkiar, etc., are some of the leading lights in the field of Kudiyattam.

Many changes have taken place in *Kudiattom* during its long history. However, as Farley Richmond enjoins, "it has survived precisely because the families of actors have doggedly preserved the tradition in an orthodox manner in the orthodox environment of the temple"[21]. Apparently, as in the case of any other artistic activity, the economic side of *Kudiattom* has not been sound. Most of the actors manage to survive by seeking alternative occupations. As Farley Richmond adds, "it certainly has not been a lucrative occupation even during the best of times. Given the critical economic plight of the actors, it could be that the future holds many more radical changes for the art, in order that its participants may sustain themselves and their families"[22].

Patayani

Patayani, is another important ritual dramatic genre of Kerala. It is performed mainly in the central Travancore region of Kerala. The staging is made in the open ground near the temples during April-May and lasts for about twenty-five days. Indications suggest that the genre was in existence during the eight century. The performance is done invariably by the members of the Kaniyan caste, the traditional astrologer community of Kerala. As a starting point, masks of areca sheaths painted in natural colours with grotesque figures of different spirits are made. In continuation, villagers who wear these masks move in a procession to the temple on the very first day of the performance. On the third day, masked dances commence propitiated with Ganapati *kolam.* Other *kolams* also appear in the scene. *Kolam* of *Kalan* is the most important among them. *Kutira,* referring to the establishment of commercial relations with Arabia in the past, is another one. Apart from the manifestation of spirits, social characters like the Brahmin land-lord with his valet and Christian ferrymen make interesting dramatic performances.

Teyyam

Teyyam, a ritual performance of antic origin is popular in the Kannur and Kasaragod districts of Kerala, and also in Coorg, and the Dakshina Kannada Districts of Karnataka state. It is performed in *Kavus*, ancestral homes, and public places, as a worshipful offering of the community for its well-being. Various communities like the Malayan, Vannan, Velan, Pulayan, Mavilan and Koppuvalan are associated with *Teyyam.* It is perhaps the only dramatic form of the lower classes of people in Kerala as other forms like *Kudiattom* and *Kathakali* were meant for upper classes to which lower classes were denied admission in the past. The main task of the *Teyyam* festival, according to Hollowman, is to create a divine reality in the human world. This is accomplished by drawing upon aesthetic and theatrical strategies like drumming, singing of sacred songs, dance movements, the wearing of elaborate costumes, and make-up, gesturing procession, feasting and the manipulation of various paraphernalia such as flags, lamps, swords, and shields. The performer is supposed to become the deity in manifest form[23]. The person who transforms into a *Teyyam* inherits the right to perform the ritual ceremony. A large number of *Teyyam* belonging to gods, goddesses, ancestral animals, serpents, trees, devils and war heroes coexist.

The enactment of the the narrative, describing the mythological story comprises the gist of *Teyyam*. As an author depicts, "the enactment does not literarily convey the narrative, but highlights the emotional content through body movement, gestures, vocal articulation, costumes and possession"[24]. The instruments accompanying *Teyyam* during the course of the performance are *chenda*, *cymbols* and *kurumkuzhal*. *Teyyam* showers blessings upon the devotees and distributes *prasadom*; the most popular of them being turmeric powder. Even toddy is distributed as *prasadom* in some cases.

The economic conditions of the genre is depicted by an author as follows:

"The performers make little money. And as Kerala continues to shift from an economy based upon exchange of services to a wage, performers are finding it increasingly difficult to make both ends meet from performing alone. Those demanding more money have met with hostility from patrons and sponsoring organisations. We know of at least one case in which a shrine discontinued its annual festival together over a discrepancy regarding how much performers should be paid. Some performers supplement their income by engaging in menial jobs as rolling cigarettes and repairing umbrellas. However, as new occupations have become more available to the larger sections of the society, Malayans and Vannans have taken up such jobs as tailoring, teaching, and banking and jobs connected with civil service. But when unemployed, many of them fall back on performing *Teyyam*"[25].

Kathakali

Kathakali is perhaps the most popular form of ritualistic performance not only in Kerala, but also in various foreign countries. Its international popularity "comes from its exuberant, heroic *tandava* style, which colours *Kathakali's* blending of dance, acting, and music. This characteristic vigorous style has been joined with a language of hand gestures, and facial expressions, as well as with colourful costuming and make-up, to create larger than life characters for the *Kathakali* stage"[26].

Kathakali as a new genre dates back to 17th century, as its probable period of origin. Its stories are known as *Attakatha,* meaning stories for acting. It is believed that prince Vira Kerala Varma of Kottaraka is the originator of *Kathakali*. He is credited with having composed the first *Attakatha* in Malayalam, a new form of dramatic script based on Ramayana towards the close of seventeenth century, then termed

Ramanattom, when Zamorin of Calicut declined to send *Krishnattom* troupe to Kottarakara. It is perhaps the first theatrical performance based on Malayalam literary texts. Subsequently, other authors enriched *Kathakali* by composing new plays. Raja of Kottayam, Unnayi Warier, Irayimman Thampi etc., are some of the leading authors, connected with Kathakali. As on today, there are over 100 surviving *Attakathas.* The stylized acting and visual representation of *Kudiyattom* and ritualistic elements of *Mudiyettam* are appropriated in *Kathakali.*

As Zarrilli adds, "these *Ramanattam* plays were a cycle of eight plays based on Ramayana reflecting the fact that they were probably modelled on *Krishnattom's* eight play cycle. The change in name to *Kathakali,* came later as *Ramanattom* expanded to include their plays outside the Ramayana and as the dance-drama evolved artistically and aesthetically"[27]. During recent years, non-epic stories including also Christian and Muslim storys appeared among *Kathakali* performances. Other changes also occurred. The speaking, or singing, of text became divorced from acting. *Kathakali* developed its distinctive energetic choreographic style, where the entire script is given to vocalist, freeing the actor-dancer for the vigorous choreography and complex gesturial interpretation of the script. Costuming and make-up also underwent changes. As Zarilli enjoins, "the emergence of a wider range of performance techniques, the consolidation of *Kathakal's* vigorous heroic, strong style, and the standardisation of costuming all combined to make *Kathakali* a highly popular, yet virtuosic, generally, by the early to mid seventeenth century"[28].

Three schools of *Kathakali* emerged in course of time, with the innovations introduced by three veterans. They are Vettethunadu representing northern, Kallattigotu representing the middle and Kaplingattu representing the southern Kerala. By establishing Kerala Kalamandalam at Cheruthurithi in 1933, Mahakavi Vallathol gave a new life to *Kathakali* and elevated it to an international stature.

Actors in *Kathakali* undergo rigorous training stretching over years. In the past actors who enrol for performance at very young age were invariably from upper castes. A wide spectrum of actors from different castes enrol for training during recent years. Even foreigners also take keen interest and perform *Kathakali* after undergoing training. Members of upper castes were the patrons of *Kathakali.* Though continuance and integrity in aesthetic and style have been maintained, process of change and modernisation are underway. The texts are mainly in Malayalam. A high proportion of Sanskrit is normally incorporated in the text.

Though *Kathakali* receives its patronage from rich families, it has been in distress. However, with the timely innovation introduced by Vallathol, state government and other voluntary bodies came forward to sustain it on healthy wicket. An interesting system of patronage exists in the performance in Sri Vallabha temple at Thiruvalla. In that temple, a devotee may commission a *Kathakali* performance as an offering to the deities of the temple. The cost of a performance runs between $83 and $100 (Rs. 1000-1200)[29].

Chavittunatakam

Kerala cannot claim for any significant contribution in the field of art and literature till the advent of modern period. Even Malayalam can trace its origin as a distinct language only from the fifteenth century. As seen earlier, *Kathakali*, the world renowned dramatic genre, has its origin since then. If at all any performances were staged earlier, they were all pure ritual performances of primitive form. The Syrian Christians of Kerala, known as Christians of serra, had very little inclination towards artistic activities of their own in those days. However, the missionary activities which ensued from the fifteenth century seemed to have instilled among the Christians a favourable inclination towards artistic activities. This was accomplished by the introduction of a new dramatic genre termed *Chavittunatakam*.

The stories of Christian heroes, Christian legends and Biblical events are presented as themes in *Chavittunatakam*. It combines the artistic style of *Kudiattom*, the ancient form of Sanskrit dramatic genre of Kerala, with European opera. In addition, the martial tradition of Kerala preserved through *Kalari Payattu* is also appropriated. *Kalaries* are training centres of the combatants who are trained in martial art under a *Guru* or *Asan*. The inspiration for including the martial element seemed to have stemmed from *Patayani*, an indigenous theatrical performance staged in temples.

Significantly, *Chavittunatakam* was introduced as a novel form of art at a time when drama as a genre was for all practical purposes unknown in Kerala. It is basically a music drama performed with rhythmic staging of foot on wooden platform as in gymnastics. For this purpose, wooden platform nearly four feet above the ground level is erected. It emerged as an important form of art in the coastal belt of Kerala where the Portuguese wielded power. It did not penetrate into the interior parts of Kerala where the Portuguese missionary activities were not sufficiently strong.

The exact origin of this form of art remains as a disputable point. According to Sabeena Raphy, an authority on *Chavittunatakam,* it had its origin exactly one hundred years before that of *Kathakali*, the world renowned dramatic genre of Kerala. She further contends, that the stage enacting *Karalmancharithram* would have been the first dramatic theatres of Kerala[30]. On the other hand, C.J. Thomas, another authority on drama, maintains that the Portuguese introduced *Chavittunatakam* for the purpose of entertaining Portuguese settlers and their offspring in and around Cochin, and he derisively labels it as *Parankikala*. Instead, Chummar Chundal, another authority, contends that *Chavittunatakam* as a genre is of Tamil origin and reached Kerala from Tamilnadu. In his opinion, *Terukkuttu* of Tamil Nadu and *Chavittunatakam* of Kerala have certain common terms and phrases which is a manifestation of Tamil connection. Interestingly, he believes that *Nadagamma*, a dramatic genre popular in Sri Lanka, resembles to a large extent, the Tamil genre *Terukuttu*. Accordingly, he contends "the texts which are used for the production of *Chavittunatakam* have come from Tamilnadu, as the by-product of missionary work. The basic rudiments of content, costume, and presentation of *Chavittunatakam* can even now be visibly traced to some of the Christian theatrical arts of Tamilnadu, as *Alannatakam*, *Muvarasunatakam* etc., have definite overtones of *Chavittunatakam* in many respects"[31]. The Tamil connection cannot be ruled out, as the missionaries moved to and fro between Kerala and Tamilnadu during those days of Portuguese hegemony in Kerala. Even if it is not an adaptation of Tamil, certain Tamil artists who happened to visit Kerala in those days would have a positive role in its development.

However, the dominant line of thinking is to attribute its origin exclusively to the endeavours of European missionaries in Kerala. The Christians were participants in all the Hindu temple festivals in the past. With the ban imposed by the Synod of Diamper in 1599 on the Christians, from participating in Hindu rituals and performances in temples, *Chavittunatakam* was introduced as an alterative genre to meet the artistic needs of the Christians in order, on the one hand, to counter the lure of Hindu ritual performances and on the other, to promote Christian teachings and tradition. Christian themes and stories were imported from Europe by the missionaries. Some artists who happened to visit Kerala at that period of time, would also have contributed their share to the making of *Chavittunatakam*. In this connection, it may be mentioned that one Chinna Thampi, who is believed to be of Tamil origin, is credited with having composed one of the early scripts of *Chavittunatakam*. Some authors believe that he was a European missionary and not a Tamilian. Whatever be its origin, it penetrated into the coastal belt of Kerala at the behest of Christian missionaries. Since the missionaries were frequently visiting Tamilnadu in those days, they themselves would have introduced the themes of European origin both in Kerala and Tamil Nadu. Whether it reached Kerala from Tamilnadu, or whether some Tamil authors who visited Cochin composed them are issues still remaining unresolved. However, there is close similarities between *Terukkkuttu*, a dramatic genre of Tamilnadu and *Chavittunatakam*. Probably the scripts of *Chavittunatakam* were composed at a time when Tamil terms were still popular in Kerala.

Chavittunatakam is very popular with the Latin Christians of Kerala who stage it during festival seasons. It is staged with utmost vigour and reverence. The audiences are not mere merry makers, but devotees to their faith, who sit throughout with rapt attention. However, it has not gained much credibility in so far as its artistic and literary qualities are concerned. In the words of K.M. George, the historian of Malayalam literature, "the use of costumes and masks as well as curtain for the stage, then introduced was novelty in Kerala. However, the literary quality of the songs and dialogues in *Chavittunatakam* were rather low. The movement of the actors on the stage arrest our attention as that of the acrobats. They are more vigorous than graceful, more martial than artistic"[32]. The veteran Malayalam dramatist G. Sankara Pillai, feels that it could not gain credibility as a dramatic genre on account of the imperfect synthesis of European themes with Indian practices[33]. There has been no attempt to upgrade the genre in the context of the innovative changes which have taken place in the field of all kinds of arts. At the same time, *Chavittunatakam* is a costly venture as in the case of any dramatic performance. It could not attract sufficient patronage from any quarter. Neither the Church, nor rich patrons, came forward to sustain it over the years. Very often, the members of the troupe themselves had to share the whole amount of expenditure and naturally it lost its economic viability.

Beginnings of Modern Dramatic Theatres in Kerala

It took nearly three centuries since the inception of *Chavittunatakam* for the appearance of modern Malayalam dramatic theatres. The hold of ritualistic tradition and the deep rooted stratification of the worst kind seem to have contributed to the delay in the appearance of drama in Kerala. The lower classes were denied to hear, let alone see the the ritualistic oriented dramatic performances staged in temple premises. New ideas conducive to the development of art and literature were yet to penetrate in Kerala. However, the establishment of British colonial system by the middle of the eighteenth century and the subsequent introduction of English education paved the way for the gradual penetration of European ideas and practices. In the meanwhile, as indicated earlier, it did not take much time for the appearance of English dramas in the cities like Calcutta, Bombay and Madras. Taking the cue from these developments, drama proper also began to appear in Kerala from the closing decades of the nineteenth century.

Three strands in the development of drama were discernible in Kerala during the formative period. The dramatic tradition of Sanskrit was not extinct in Kerala. *Kudiattom* is a shining example of this tradition, not only in Kerala, but also the whole of India. A new development which ensued throughout India was the translation of the old Sanskrit dramas of the past into various Indian languages. Thus the translation of *Shakuntalam* and other classical dramas to various vernacular languages of India became the order of the day. Translation of different Sanskrit works began to appear in Malayalam also. The ball was set in motion, by Valia Koil Thampuran who translated *Vijnanasakuntalam* in 1882. Initially, the work of Koil Thampuran was not staged as it was written with an overdose of Sanskrit vocabulary. It could be staged with acclaim throughout Kerala once Thampuran himself modified it with the liberal insertion of Malayalam vocabulary. It was enacted in different places with the leading stars of the day appearing as different characters. Even before Koil Thapuran's translation, Sri Ayilam Thirunal, the then ruling king of Travancore, had also translated another work, though not actually published immediately. Many other works were translated into Malayalam by different authors of the period.

Works in Malayalam on the model of Sanskrit drama also began to appear around this time. They were oriented towards poetic qualities, rather than with performance style. It is attributed "to the dominance of theatrical forms like *Kathakali* which could fulfil the theatrical urges of the upper classes in general"[34]. The authors were aware of such situation. Kodungallur Kunhikuttan Thampuran, Thottakkattu Madhaviamma, Kochippan Tharakan, Kodungallur Kochunnithampuran and Kandathil Varghese Mappillai, were some of the prominent authors who enriched dramatic literature during that period by writing dramatic works. It is reported that Kochippan Tharakan had actually written *Mariamma*, a dramatic work in 1878, prior to the publication of any other Malayalam drama. He could, however publish it only in 1903[35]. Kollam Narayana Pillai, Mattom Kochukunju Baghavatar, Attingal Neelakanda Pillai, Karukathil Kesava Pillai, etc., were some of the leading actors who staged the performances during those days of Malayalam drama[36].

The arrival of itinerant Tamil dramatic troupes and the staging of drama in various centres of Kerala is another development. Tamil artists who were inspired by the success of commercial dramas in Bombay opened commercial theatres in Tamilnadu and successfully staged many performances. In turn, a large number of successful troupes like Kalyanaraman set, Ramudu set, Swami Iyer set and Babalan Kuttiswaran set moved into Kerala with their band of popular stars and staged the performances in various parts of Kerala. S.V. Subbiah, S.R. Janaki, Kittappa, Alvar, K.V. Sundarambal and Ratnabai were some of the leading actors who entertained Malayalees with their histrionic skill in the plays. Though deficient in thematic qualities, their music drama style was indeed a novel form of performance. The lavish display of colourful costumes in combination with skilful histrionic talents of the actors intermingled with melodious songs could satisfy the entertainment needs of the audience in all centres where they were staged. It was, they who introduced the commercial element in dramatic theatres by collecting entrance fee by selling tickets for seeing the performance.

Inspired by the success of the Tamil troupes, Malayalee authors also started to compose scripts of music-drama (*sangeetha natakam*) genre on the model of the Tamil version. Large number of audiences greeted the performances which fetched buoyant box office collections in all centres where they were staged. T.C. Achutha Menon stands foremost as a leading author of music-drama in Malayalam. His dramatic work, *Sangeethaoushadam* published in 1892, is perhaps the first work of this model in Malayalam. It was an excellent literary piece whose 35000 copies were sold in no time[37]. Equally successful was its staging as a drama in attracting large number of audience. K.C. Kesava Pillai was an equally gifted script writer whose work '*Saradamma*' (1903) won acclaim in no time. It could also attract large number of audience wherever it was staged. They are noted for the adoption of pure vernacular Malayalam rather than the highly Sanskritised Malayalam of the past. *Kuruppilaakkalari* of C.V. Raman Pillai was another important wok in pure Malayalam. In the words of Ramachandran, "the verse form of this performance pattern which developed slowly, was very much based on the vernacular Malayalam with its highly flexible metrical pattern and this was really a major break- through in the performance history of Kerala"[38].

Translation of English dramas was the third strand in the development of Malayalam drama during its formative stage. Works of Shakespeare, Moliere, etc., were translated into Malayalam by authors like Kallur Oommen Philipose, Kandathil Varghese Mappillai, C. Govindan, Kodungallur Kunhikuttan Thampuran, Diwan Bahadur A. Govinda Pillai, etc. Thus Malayalam version of *Merchant of Venice, Taiming of the Shrew, Tempest, Comedy of Errors*, etc., appeared around this time.

Another offshoot of the development was the slow emergence of a new theatrical culture. The performances of the past were merely rituals staged in the temple premises during festival seasons. With the spread of education, an urge for entertainment began to take shape in the minds of the middle classes. When the staging of Tamil dramas and Malayalam dramas commenced, large number of people who were eager for entertainment flooded the theatres. Ticket charges varied from one *Chakram* to floor seat, four *Chakrams* to bench and ten *Chakrams* to VIP seats during the first half of twentieth century[39]. The rates were fairly high according to the then standatds. However, the dramatic companies evinced very little interest to understand the inclination of the audience. Unfortunately as Sankara Pillai adds, "neither an attempt to understand the inclinations of the audience, nor to convert the audience into a proper appreciative class both by the Tamil dramatic troupes and the local dranmatic troupes alike"[40].

Opening of professional dramatic companies was on the anvil in close succession to the newfound interest for drama. Manomohanam, a dramatic company, started by Tiruvattur Narayana Pillai in south Travancore, followed by Rasikaranjini of Chathukutty Mannadiar in central Kerala, Vinodachinthamani of C.P. Achutha Menon, and Paramavilasom Company of P.S. Nair were some of the earlier professional companies opened in close succession. It is reported that rhere were well over 32 dramatic troupes operating in Kerala during the hey-day of *sangeetha natakam*[41]. Within the next fifteen to twenty years, more than two hundred plays were performed through out the length and breadth of Kerala[42]. As in the case of Tamil dramas, the lavish display of spectacles, clothing and skillfull acting, were the notable features of the plays. Most ofthe theatres where dramas were enacted were crude in nature with very little facilities for proper staging. Similarly, most of the dramatic literature were devoid of intrinsic qualities. By and large, they were mere imitations of the commercial drama of Tamil.

Changing Contours of Malayalam Drama

Dramatic works in Malayalam were nurtured by Sanskrit, Tamil and English tradition during the formative stage. In fact, they were highly influenced by the literature and structural formation of the works of those languages. As years went by, dramatists began to chalk out independent path by distancing themselves from those influences. One of the first steps taken was to focus on social issues and utilise drama as an agent of change in society. Drama began to reflect social reality and asserted as a corrective force. Progressive ideas inculcated in society by the spread of education accounted for such changes.

The pioneer in opening a new path on those lines in Malayalam drama was V.T. Bhattathiripad, a Namboodiri Brahmin, who was dissatisfied with the oppressive system which kept Namboodiri women in perpetual bondage. He was a progressive thinker who formed the Namboodiri Yoga Samithi which wanted to reform the Namboodiri community by abolishing the evil practices and thereby to free Namboodiri women from the clutches of the oppressive system. Through his script *Adukkalayil ninnu Arangathekku*, he portayed the miserable conditions of Namboodiri women and advocated the need for redeeming them. M.R.B., another social reformer, through his dramatic work *Marakkukudakkullile Mahanarakam*, projected what Bhattathiripd advocated with much more vigour and sincerity of purpose. Another dramatist, Premji elaborated the issue with new hindsights through his work *Wruthumati.*

The approach of these authors was to give priority to theme rather than to the characters. What they did was to project the oppressive conditions prevailing in society and then to present the story in which key roles were earmarked to appropriate characters. Kesari Balakrishna Pillai and C. Narayana Pillai, who followed them, accelerated the process further. The inquisitive spirit of rationalism which gained ascendancy in Europe was also reflected in the dramatic works of the period. As an author says, "thus the vigorous and socially meaningful period in the history of Malayalam performance began for the first time in Kerala from the last phase of the twenties"[43].

Another significant development was the adoption of Ibsen's approach in Malayalam drama. A notable instance is the portrayal of tragic endings as a natural outcome of human existence by the dramatists of the period. The people who associated with such a trend were N. Krishna Pillai, K.T. Mohammad, Thoppil Bhasi, C.N. Srikandan Nair and G. Sankara Pillai. Such thematic and structural orientation are well reflected in *Bhagmana, Kanyaka, Balabalam, Darshanam, Anuranjanam, Mudakkumuthal*, and so on. Another dramatic genius of the period was C.J. Thomas. He was an original dramatist who could make lasting impression in the history of Malayalam drama, though he wrote only two or three works.

Close on the heels of these developments was the birth of a new dramatic movement. A beginning was made with the formation of the Indian Theatre Association around 1940. The Kerala People's Theatre Arts Club (KPAC) was established on the model of Indian Theatre Association. These associations were basically political theatres, which took up the cause of the down- trodden classes, and also provided additional leverage to the freedom movement.

In Kerala, the leading light of the movement was Thoppil Bhasi. In fact, K. Damodaran through his work *Pattabakki,* has been the pioneer of the movement in Kerala. However, it was Thoppil Bhasi who widened the base through his performances. Credit should go to him for having successfully integrated Indian dramatic tradition, with the local cultural heritage and the burning problems confronting the society in a proper dramatic style. He has composed over thirty scripts, and successfully staged them. His *Ningalenne Communistacky* stands as a masterpiece. It was a cultural product whose contribution in strengthening Communist movement in Kerala is significant. Equally successful was his endeavour to follow an independent dramatic style, differing both from the Aristotelian and Ibsen tradition. He was able to portray the voice of the oppressed and chalk out an opening for their liberation. While KPAC under the stewardship of Thoppil Bhasi was staging popular dramas in Travancore, Malabar Kendra Kala Samithi was growing as a powerful progressive theatrical movement in Malabar. Side by side, commercial theatrical practices were serving the trivial entertainment needs of the masses.

Proliferation of Works during the Post-Independence Period

By the time of independence, Malayalam drama could chalk out an independent path freeing itself from the Tamil and Sanskrit tradition. What followed was the appearance of a wide variety of dramatic works by a host of authors. They touched on all aspects of life, by presenting them in various dramatic models. Among the authors, who enriched Malayalam drama during the post-independence period, mention may be made of K.T. Mohammad, N. Krishna Pillai, C.N. Srikandan Nair,

Cherukadu, G. Sankara Pillai, T.N. Gopinathan Nair, C.L. Jose, Thikkodian, Kainikkara brothers, P.K. Vikraman Nair, P.J. Antony and so on. Most of them were connected with amateurist theatre. However, some among them like K.T. Mohammad and C.N. Srikandan Nair were associated with professional theatres also. Most of the works of the period were staged successfully in the theatres spread throughout Kerala. Notable works written by them include, *Chuvanna Ghadikaram* by K.T. Mohammad, *Velicham Vilakkanwashikkunnu, Tharavaditham* of Cherukadu, *Nashtakachavatom* of C.N. Srikandan Nair, *Kannadi, Gurudakshina, Railppalangal* of G. Sankara Pillai, etc., which were staged in different theatres, though originally meant for amateur stage.

One of the significant development of the latter half of twentieth century was the realisation of the need for education and training in acting. Drama deserves to be regarded as a profession, as any other professional activity which relies on skill development for their success. The opening of the School of Drama at Delhi was the first step taken in this regard at the national level. The need for imparting training was recognised as sound policy for the development of drama in Kerala also. The convening of the dramatic *kalary* at Sasthamcotta at the initiative of Srikandan Nair, G. Sankara Pillai and others was the first step in that direction. In close succession, seminars and work shops were organised in different places. The starting of the School of Drama at Trichur, under the University of Calicut, was the culmination of those developments. Formal training in acting, in combination with lessons for appreciation, are the main academic activities of the School. Similar schools to impart training in drama were started in other Universities also. The School at Trichur, under the stewardship of G. Sankara Pillai, who himself is one of the foremost dramatists of Kerala with a plethora of works, has done yeomen service to the healthy development of drama as an academic activity.

A new development in the history of drama is the movement for incorporating the indigenous performances with the main dramatic tradition. Indigenous dramatic genres are popular in most of the countries of the world. During recent years, many authors of Kerala have come forward to give expression to the indigenous genres in their writings. Kavalam Narayana Panicker, is perhaps the most prominent among them. He draws on the regional musical, dance, ritual and martial art form the *kalaripayattu*, to create his own dramatic genre. Most of his writings, staged successfully, not only in Kerala but also in other parts of India, are modelled on the indigenous tradition. His work, *Karimkutty* is perhaps the most popular dramatic script which portrays the life of the downtrodden classes in the past in graphic detail. In conformity to Indian tradition, he gives priority to acting in the stage than to the literary style. As Vayala Vasudevan Pillai enjoins, "he has succeeded in giving primacy to the performances rather than to the literary qualities"[44]. In other words, the bodily movements of the actor constitute the language of expression. Dharwadker goes further, and states that "three concepts are especially pertinent to a discussion of his method, – his interest in the universal language of the theatre, his classically derived definition of theatre as "visual poetry" and his understanding of the theatrical text as an occasion for non-textual staging"[45]. Sopanam, his dramatic school, the locus of action of his theatrical concepts, remains as a citadel of theatrical drama unscathed by the mediated drama of the culture industry. At the same time, he stands tallest among the dramatists in Malayalam with an all India stature.

Another equally important development in Kerala is the emergence of women dramatic theatres. It was men, who dominated the dramatic field of Kerala during the early stages of its evolution both as writers and actors alike. A change is in the offing with the growth of the feminist movement. As stated earlier, the objective of the writings of Bhattathiripad has been the liberation of Namboodiri women. In succession, women authors have come to the stage by writing their own scripts. Lalithambka Antharjanam, Srija, etc., are some of the leading writers.

Street dramas which became popular in many parts of India had its echo in Kerala also. G. Sankara Pillai, K.J. Baby, John Abraham, Karivellur Murali, etc., are associated with street drama in Kerala.

A galaxy of actors enriched Malayalam dramatic theatres over the years. Some of the prominent among them who enriched the stage during recent years are Oduvil Unnikrishnan, K.P.A.C. Leela, Jamal Kochangadi, Jayaprakas Kulur, Leela Koothattukulam, K.P.A.C. Lalitha, Saithan Joseph, Paravoor Devarajan, Kodungallur Amminiyamma, Changanacherry Natarajan, Nilambur Aisha, Sundaran Kallayi, Adoor Pankajam, Kuttiyedatyi Vilasini, Paravoor George, Ebrahim Vengara, Vikraman Nair, K.M. Dharman, Kozhikode Santha Devi, Rajan P. Dev, Vettakulam Sivanandan, Cochin Varghese, etc. Some among them have migrated to the film world also. Significantly, most of the film stars in Malayalam had their innings in the world of dramatic theatres.

The fifties saw the erosion of the base of drama with the upsurge of Malayalam cinema. There was a growing apprehension that drama may not be able to hold on against the onslaught of cinema. Though drama could weather the storm, another threat which can even erode the foundations of drama has appeared. It is the spectacular growth of television which has penetrated throughout the world by offering dramatic performance free of cost. The impact of those technologically mediated drama on theatrical drama would be uncovered in the Chapters that follow.

NOTES AND REFERENCES

1. Jain Nemichandra (1992); *Indian Thetre Tradition, Continuity and Change* (New Delhi, Vikas Publishing House) p. 25.
2. Jain Nemichandra (1992); *op. cit.*, p. 14.
3. Solomen Rakesh. H. (2009); "Towards a Geneology of Indian Theatre Historiography" in Bhatia Nandi (ed.); *Modern Indian Theatre: A Reader* (New Delhi, Oxford University Press) p. 4.
4. quoted by Jain Nemichandra (1992); *op. cit.*, p. 15.
5. Quoted by Richmond Farley (ed.) (1993); *Indian Theatre: Traditions of Performance* (Delhi, Motilal Publishers), p. 26.
6. Jain Nemichandra (1992); *op. cit.*, p. 27.
7. Richmond Farley (ed.) (1993); *Indian Theatre: Traditions of Performance* (Delhi Motilal Banarsida Publishers, Private Ltd.), p. 80.
8. Jain Nemichandra (1992); *op. cit.*, p. 40.
9. Jain Nemichandra (1992); *op. cit.*, p. 50.
10. Jain Nemichandra (1992); *op. cit.*, p. 70.
11. Gokhale Shanta; 'Marathi Theatre' in Lal Anand (2009); *Theatres in India: A Concise Companion* (Delhi, Oxford University Press), p. 82.
12. Jain Nemichandra (1992); *op. cit.*, p. 72.
13. Jain Nemichandra (1992); *op. cit.*, p. 77.
14. Jain Nemichandra (1992); *op. cit.*, p. 80.
15. Nagabhushana Sarma. M. (2009); "Telugu Theatre" in Lal Anand; *op. cit.*, p. 151.
16. *Ibid.*
17. Jain Kirti (2009); "Hindi Theatre" in Lal Anand; *op. cit.*, p. 47.
18. Jain Kirti (2009) in Lal Anand; *op. cit.*, p. 45.
19. Farley Richmond *et al.* (1993); *Indian Theatre: Tradition of Perormance* (Delhi, Motilal Banarsidass Publishers) p. 87.
20. K.N. Panicker; "*Kudiattom*" in Lal Anand (2009); *Theatres in India: A Consise Companion* (New Delhi, Oxford University Press), p. 279.
21. Richmond Farley (1993); *op. cit.*, p. 115.
22. Richmond Farley (1993); *op. cit.*, p. 116.
23. Ashley Wayne and Hollowman Regina (1993); "Teyyam" in Richmond Farley; *op. cit.*, p. 131.
24. K.N. Panicker (2009); "Teyyam" in Lal Anand (2009); *op. cit.*, p. 415.
25. Ashley Wayne and Hollowman Regina (1993); *op. cit.*, p. 135.
26. Zarrilli Philip. B. (1993); *Kathakali* in Richmond Farley; *op. cit.*, p. 315.

27. Zarilli, Phiilip B. (1993); *op. cit.*, p. 317.
28. Zarilli, Philip B. (1993); *op. cit.*, p. 318.
29. Richmond, Farley (1993); *op. cit.*, pp. 429-30.
30. Raphy, Sabina (1969); *Chavittunatakam* (Kottayam NBS) p. 16.
31. Choondal Chummar (1984); *Christian Theatre in India* (Thrissur, St. Thomas I.S. Press) p. 77.
32. Choondal, Chummar (1984) quotes from K.M. George (1968); *A Survey of Malayalam Literature* (New Delhi,), p. 191.
33. Pillai G. Sankara (1991): *History of Malyalam Dramatc Literature* (Thrissur, Kerala Sahitya Acadmy) p. 25.
34. Ramachandran, V.M. (2001); "The Modern Malayalam Theatre" in Cherian P.J. (ed.), *Essays on the Cutural Formation of Kerala* (Trivandrum, K.C.H.R. Publications) p. 3.
35. *Malayala Manorama* (Malayalam daily, Kottayam, dated 09-08-2015).
36. Vayala, Vasuden Pillai (2005); *Malayala Nataka Sahithyacharthram* (History of Malayalam Dramatic Literature Thrissur, Kerala Sahitya Academy) p. 17.
37. Vayala, Vasudevan Pillai (2005); *Malayala Nataka Sahityacharithram* (Mal-*History of Malyalam Dramatic Literature*) (*Thrissur, Kerala Sahitya Academy*) p. 23.
38. Ramachandran, V.M. (3001); *op. cit.*, p. 5.
39. *Chakram* was a coin in circulation in the princely state of Travancore. It was equal to 1/28 of an Indian Rupee. See also Sreekumar. K. (2002); *Malayala Sangeetha Nataka Charithram* (Kozhikode, Poorna Publications) pp. 358-61.
40. Sankara, Pillai G. (1991); *op. cit.*, p. 38.
41. Sreekumar, K. (2002); *op. cit.*, pp. 318-19.
42. Ramachandran, V.M. (2001); *op. cit.*, p. 6.
43. Ramachandran, V.M. (2001); *op. cit.*, p. 7.
44. Vayala, Vasudevan Pillai (2005): *op. cit.*, p. 128.
45. Dharwadker, Aparna Bhargava (2005); *Theatre of Independence* (New Delhi, Oxford University Press) p. 103.

5

Production Units, Costs and Returns of Stage Drama

In previous Chapters, we have seen the evolution of drama over the years as a joint cultural activity in which a few artists join together to produce, or perform, the drama, an important artistic genre, in live form. Since drama, per se, is an artistic product created with the aid of both material and artistic inputs, it becomes a Janus–faced joint cultural activity, which calls for some kind of organisational arrangement to link the inputs as a unit to engage in the productive activity. What type of organisational arrangements are operating in the dramatic world comes to the fore as an important question. Since a dramatic performance is a joint venture of various artistic and material inputs, cost becomes an important feature of any drama in the live form. In what proportion, different components of the costs are incurred for a drama, forms another question. How drama meets the cost poses as another question. In this Chapter answers to these questions are sought by drawing evidences from Malayalam drama.

Contract between Art and Commerce

As a cultural genre, drama is concerned with the enactment of a story in live form. Actors representing different characters appear in the scene in conformity to the requirements of the story. Usually, one leading male and a female actor assume key roles in any drama. Supporting actors both males and females would be required to complete the story with a sense of reality. Music and dance, invariably in the recorded form also will make the scenes more appealing. The story itself would be composed in such a way as to express the events in a lively form. The dialogue or script termed drama in the ordinary parlance which bestows immortality to drama in many instances forms yet another input. Dramatic performances are staged in an elevated platform very often inside a theatre.

They are staged in front of an audience who are to be seated comfortably. Material inputs in the form of make-up materials, costumes, scenery, light, sound, ordinary labour, etc., are also needed for a dramatic performance. Actors in a drama have to be trained before staging the play. Apparently, material and non-material inputs enter in different proportions in any dramatic performance. Thus drama is enacted in live form in front of an audiences who become the consumers of the product. It is not a complete product but a process of performance.

Since drama is a cultural product with unique quality, total uncertainty looms large regarding the capacity of a particular performance to satisfy the tastes of the audience, the purchaser. At the same time, the artists who create the product are not in a position to market the product. Apparently, an understanding of the modus operandi of artistic production and marketing becomes difficult under such circumstances. The problem is glaring even in the case of dramtic production on commercial lines. In the light of such a predicament, the theatrical formulation of Caves, which he subsumed under the rubric of creative industries becomes handy for understanding the problem. He, in his book *Contract between Art and Commerce,* has provided elaborate details on the modus operandi of contract between art and commerce in the creative industry.

What transpires in the creative industry, is the creation of cultural goods with the artists assuming key role as producers. However, the value of cultural products remain indeterminate till it is marketed. Moreover, the artists by themselves may not be in a position to secure a fair return for the products in the market. In turn, the artists have to enlist the support of non-cultural inputs which Caves calls humdrum. As he visualises, the artist needs a gallery to display and promote works to potential purchasers. Similarly, the author of a book requires a publisher and the pop musician a record label. In brief, each creative activity demands a diverse group, as well as a set of humdrum inputs. The humdrum inputs by themselves are incapable of producing cultural products which the artists alone are capable of producing or creating it. As a way out, the artists and the humdrum inputs enter into some kind of contract. In his own words, "the question of how contracts work between art and commerce thus is nested within the larger question of why artists and humdrum inputs choose to structure their relationship as they do"[1]. Being parties to the contract, their relationship resembles to that of a joint venture. As he adds further, "the artist's creative spark may be necessary to the dealer's success, but so is the dealer's promotional effort to the artists renown and each party's action affects the benefit flowing to the other"[2]. Thus the two parties operating from two angles with altogether different motivations come to a contract for making a gain.

The contracting phenomenon becomes all the more important in the case of a drama as it is an artistic product stemming from a joint venture within the premises of a theatre by artistic and non-artistic inputs. As Hamilton adds, "but there is one of the arts, – the art of drama – can never be disassociated from its concomitant business, – the business of the theatre"[3]. Contractual arrangements encompassing a host of artistic and non-artistic inputs within the premises of a theatre presupposes the existence of an economic organisation. As Hamilton enjoins further, "the mere existence of a theatre, a company of actors, an audience assembled, necessitates an economic organisation and presupposes a business manager; and this business manager, who sets the play before the public and attracts the public to the play, must necessarily exert a potent influence over the playwright. The only way in which a dramatist may free himself from this influence is by managing his own company"[4]. Some dramatists like Moliere or even Shakespeare for example, have managed their own business. Thus, organisational arrangements are of crucial importance for the very purpose of staging any drama in front of the audience in a theatre. It is through the organisational arrangements that the artists of different calibre are brought together to stage the performance. At the same time, the contractual mechanism is effectively managed through the organisational arrangement.

The organisational arrangement coming in the picture for the production of any commodity is known as firm in the economic jargon. Even single proprietorship also operates as a firm, since different inputs have to be organised in different proportions to produce the commodity. Large scale organisations like partnership or joint stock companies or corporate bodies undertake production with more than one firm in the fray. Firms arrange the marketing of the product also. However, the firms which produce cultural services may not always operate with a motive for profit and there can be different forms of organisations, with many of them operating as non-profit organisations.

Throsby's Three-fold Model of Production Units

However, Caves has not elaborated the nature of the organisation which turns out drama, a cultural product in live form. Since cultural products are creative in the sense that they produce cultural value, in addition to economic value, the organisations which come in the picture as producing units of cultural goods should have certain distinct characteristics. Based on the motivation of artists which guides their attitude towards remuneration for creating cultural products, Throsby, as indicated in Chapter 1, has introduced a three-fold model in the organisational arrangements for cultural production. The three- fold model seems to be suitable to explain the distinct characteristics of the organisational units which produce drama and many other forms of cultural products.

As already stated, any cultural endeavour is a creative activity which creates cultural value, distinct from economic value. The broader cultural worth denoting intrinsic aesthetic or artistic qualities stands for cultural value. Needless to say, it is the efforts of the artists which create cultural value in such cases. In the words of Throsby, "cultural value is instilled into the creative works by creative artists who respond to the mysterious leaps of the imagination and transform these stimuli into images, words or sounds – this is a process of 'forming flows of value': the artist's role is to concentrate them into a configuration which will in due course display them to the world"[5]. However, the artist does not produce in the vacuum. Instead, economic considerations in the form of income enter in the picture as important constraints as artists need money to live and other material inputs to create value. Accordingly, three types of organisational arrangement can be thought of in such creative activities. They are classified under the headings: (i) income constraint, (ii) income as a joint maximand, and (iii) income as sole maximand[6].

In the first instance, artist may require a minimum amount of income to remain in the productive activity. Such a minimum is needed not as an incentive, but as a minimum needed for creating cultural value. He believes that this type of model is broadly applicable to most works in the so-called non-commercial theatre, to classical music and to much of opera, jazz and poetry[7]. However, such a situation resembles an ideal condition like the realm of wise-men, or men of head of Plato. Such situations are rare in the actual world. In his opinion, for many artists the demand for material goods extends beyond the basic subsistence needs required for survival. They may demand more income to provide not only for higher standards of food, clothing, housing, etc., but also for access to all other goods and services which income and wealth make possible. Their artistic practice which can lead to financial reward is more than mere passing interest to them and the generation of income is far more significant. The objective function of this model can be restated as the joint maximisation of the cultural and economic value arising from the work. The model of artistic production, wherein economic and cultural value enter as joint maximands could be applied as he visualises to some fiction, some film making, some visual arts and crafts, some musical and a significant amount of popular music. Apparently, most forms of drama which require material as well as intellectual inputs can be thought of as falling within the ambit of this model.

There can be instances where artists and cultural producers are in the field solely for monetary consideration. Though their product may contain cultural value, maximisation of cultural value is not their primary motive. Instead "the weight of cultural value in the objective function dwindles to zero and the maximisation of economic value becomes the prime, if not the sole motive for creativity"[8]. On the basis of his line of tinking, this model is likely to be applicable to folk and tourist art, much of film, commercial television and popular music. Apparently, the technologically mediated drama comes within the fold of this model. Thus three types organisational arrangements can be theoretically feasible in so far as dramatic activities are concerned.

Different Categories of Dramatic Theatres

The term dramatic theatres as stated in Chapter 1, stands also as the organisational arrangement or unit of production of live drama. They are broadly divided into commercial and artistic entities. As a class, commercial theatre operates mainly to make money. Such concerns produce dramas in such a way as to make maximum gains. Theatres, which do not stand for profit making, are known as artistic theatres. The tendency for organising dramatic theatres on commercial lines for making profit is very strong in comparison with other forms of art. However, drama is a creative activity producing services which have cultural and economic value. Apparently, the term commercial does not augur well with an artistic activity like drama. Nor does the artists, by inclination like to be labelled under the term commercial. Instead, they brand such theatres which operate for profit as professional. As Farley Richmond echoes, "although they may wish to derive their living from theatre, many theatre artists consider it an insult to be called commercial and prefer instead to be labelled professional"[9]. The term professional is thus adopted as actors themselves prefer to be called professionals, as in the case of other professions. Apparently, the rationality for such a line of thinking stems from the desire to include drama also in the category of professions like medicine or engineering. They are supposed to earn sufficient income from their own profession.

Theatre which is not concerned solely with such commercial considerations are termed amateur. There are a wide range of amateur groups; viz, those that are appendages to larger groups, those that are independent and those that are educational institutions. Needless to say, most of them are organised as non-profit art groups, producing dramas which contain both artistic and economic value. A typical amateur theatre operates with a dynamic leader surrounded by a band of devoted actors. As Farley Richmond enjoins, "historically most amateur groups depend on the vision and guidance of a strong director. He brings a sense of unity and purpose to the activities of the group"[10]. The actors themselves would be of different categories seeking a career in such theatres for different reasons. Some of them who enter in the dramatic field as a stepping stone for the advancement of their career invariably begin their innings in the amateur camp. Similarly, those who are motivated by an artistic career opt themselves in the amateur theatres. Most of them may not be getting sufficient income for livelihood by participating in such units. They would in such cases regard acting as a part time calling and may take up alternative occupations.

Experimental group is another category which in some cases are mere extension of the amateur group. They are known by different names. The British refer it as the "fringe". The Swedes use the term 'free theatre', the Dutch 'experimental', and the French 'theatres engagis' or 'marge' and the Germans speak 'cellar theatre'. Many units may not be experimental in the strict sense as they are by no means all committed; "they perform in attics as often as in cellars and sometimes in the streets". Nevertheless, they do provide an alternative to the mainstream theatre[11]. The support to the experimental theatres comes mainly from the educated.

Non-profit organisation, or theatre, is a term which frequently surfaces in the literatue on drama. Any organisation which seeks to fulfil some social purpose and which does not seek pecuniary gain from the enterprise normally fall within the category of non –profit organasations. They take pride in the quality of the products. Most of the amateur theatres and experimental theatres and even a few professional theatres fall within the category of non-profit theatres.

As mentioned in Chapter 4, when dramatic theatres appeared in India during the modern period, most of them were organised on commercial lines. At present, they are not numerous in India, apparently on account of the onslaught of the mediated drama. Most of them operate as subsidiaries to other concerns for securing better returns. Within the country, Calcutta has the largest number of commercial theatres, with Mumbai and Chennai falling far behind. Even then, most of the theatres in Calcutta numbering about 3000 are being organised within amateur category. Many of them were organised as group theatres. Group theatre as Richmond Farley puts, "prides itself on performing plays that generally have a serious content, many of them satiric, and that espouse mild to strong political messages.—Although most of the workers in Calcutta's group theatre do not earn a living participating in production, they do pride themselves on the quality of their work"[12].

On the other hand, there were well over 500 amateur theatres in Bombay alone and another twenty-five hundred in Maharastra state. As in Calcutta, the group, ranges from organisations with long standing reputation for high quality of work to college theatricals. As in Calcutta, the Maharastrian middle classes love theatre, but various economic factors prevent the growth of full-time professional theatre. Calcutta is reputed for being the formost centre of experimental theatres also in India. Badal Sircar, a well known playwright and actor, has been a leading light of experimental theatre in India. As a general rule, theatrical organisations are either autonomous bodies or extensions of other organisations. Most of the theatres depend on strong personalities and teams of dedicated workers.

There are well over 1437 theatre troupes operating in Kerala at present. Of them professional theatres number 139 and amateur group 1298. They are scattered throughout the state. The Kalanilayam Vistavision Dramascope Company with its headquarters at Trivandrum has been a leading commercial theatre which used to spend most of its time on the road, travelling throughout the state. The Kerala People's Arts Company and Kalidasa Kalakendra are two major commercial concerns which have staged many plays in the past. Though there are well over 1000 amateur theatres in Kerala, they have not made any lasting impression in the state. Kerala on the other hand, can take credit for having a lively experimental theatre which stages dramas in traditional form. It is Sopanam, a theatrical troupe, owned and directed by Kavalam Narayana Panicker who could make a name for his theatre.

The organisational structure and financial arrangements of theatrical concerns in Kerala resembles to what Chummar Chundal describes about *Chavittunatakam* on which reference was made in Chapter 4. He states as follows:

> "Since the organisation of the troupe involves high expenditure, it naturally follows that the respectable and financially sound families of the Christian community of the Latin rite are the early producers of *Chavittunatakam*. They entrust the responsibility of the production, rehearsal, selection of actors, to the *asan* who is in charge of the *Kalari*. The local *Asan* gives training to the actors in the village where he gets an invitation

> for performances. If he fails to get actors for the drama, he invites artistes from other villages. Individuals move from troupe to troupe. The majority of the troupes do not have organisational set up. The troupes may be formed or disbanded. Nevertheless, the troupe is the semi-permanent unit around which the theatre organises itself. Every troupe has one or two directors [*asans*], many performers, singers, instrumentalists and back stage workers"[13].

Similarly, most of the dramas are staged under the umbrella of an organisation of some kind or other. Well established troupes have a band of permanent artists and other workers under their banner. Such well organised troupes are on the way out as dramas are becoming less remunerative. Most of the troupes are ad-hoc arrangements which stage one or two dramas in an year.

Components of the Cost

As stated earlier, dramas are staged in a theatre with the active participation of different inputs in varying proportions under the banner of a troupe. Since different inputs enter in the picture, cost for securing their services of varying nature becomes inevitable. Important among such costs are; cost for the cast, cost for supporting artists like musicians and dancers, make up materials, cost for light, sound, etc., rent for the building, cost for training, transport cost, cost for ordinary labour etc. In addition payment has to be made to the literary artist, who writes a narrative of an event or development in running dialogue. Dialogue should be in such a way as to give verbal expression to the acting. Gifted authors alone are in a position to write lively dialogue suitable for acting. Many of them, as in the case of Thoppil Bhasi, or G. Sankara Pillai, have been directors as well as master actors. Talented actors may also direct the drama, and directing becomes an important input in any drama. However, it is the actors who form an important input which renders life to any drama through the histrionic skill of the actors displayed in talk, body language, facial expression etc. In addition, musicians and dancers make drama more lively and entertaining. Costs have to be incurred for getting the services of all these inputs. Costs on cast, supporting artists, director, the script writer, and musicians and dancers fall exclusively as artistic costs and others as normal economic costs which include many items. One of them would be the cost for rehearsal of the drama which calls for food and accommodation to the actors for a few days. Furthermore, different kinds of make up materials and costumes are required for creating some sort of reality in the acting. Equipments and instruments of different kinds are also required. Any drama requires a stage and the theatre facilitates the same. Audience have to be accommodated with convenient seating arrangements. Rent to the theatre becomes an inevitable item in the cost. Similarly, labour input required to decorate the stage or arrange various activities connected with dramatic performance also calls for a fairly high cost. All such items of cost form the humdrum elements of Caves. Compared to the other arts, the cost of production of a drama is very high on account of the utilisation of a wide variety of various inputs.

A survey was made in November-December 2014, among a few dramatic troupes to collect information on the cost incurred on different items, for the staging of a few dramas by such units. A word of caution is to be made regarding the accuracy of data relating to costs and returns of drama. Most of the theatre troupes are not in the habit of keeping the accounts relating to the cost of staging a drama. They spend the money in a haphazard manner. Secondly, at least some among them may try to purify black money. Most of the artists do not receive regular payments for acting. Many of them render it as a voluntary service. Calculation and accounting of cost become difficult in the case of dramatic performances for those reasons. Though information was collectd from 20 performances, the data about most of them were of a clumsy nature. We were therefore compelled to take the details of about five performances which were found satisfactory for the purpose of analysis, though the data lack proper accounting standards.

Table 5.1 gives the distribution of costs incurred for the services of different inputs in staging five dramatic performances, which belong to different categories. While drama A and B fall within the category of amateur, C within the category of experimental, D and E within the category of professional dramas. Usually, the dramatic companies prepare one drama and stage them for a few days in a station, or different stations. In so doing, the cost of certain items like script, costumes, make up materials, training, recorded music etc., which are in the nature of fixed costs can be distributed. Actors' salary, rent and running expences have to be incurred afresh for each performance.

As can be seen from the Table, there is wide variation in the total cost. The cost varied from Rs. 1.75 lakh in the case of drama B to Rs. 4.44 lakh in the case of drama E. The cost of drama D which accounted for Rs. 334700, was equally high. Variations in the cost from drama to drama occurred on account of the difference in the nature of the story, the number

Table 5.1: Components of the Cost of a Few Dramatic Performances (in Rupees)

Item	*Drama A*	*Drama B*	*Drama C*	*Drama D*	*Drama E*
Story	25000 (9.96)	20000 (11.42)	nil	40000 (11.95)	60000 (13.51)
Cast	nil	nil	nil	14700 (4.39)	14000 (3.15)
Music	5000 (1.99)	20000 (11.42)	15000 (9.37)	35000 (10.45)	45000 (10.13)
Direction	20000 (7.96)	20000 (11.42)	30000 (18.75)	40000 (11.95)	50000 (10.26)
Dancer	5000 (1.99)	10000 (5.71)	10000 (6.25)	10000 (2.98)	20000 (4.50)
Make-up man	5000 (1.99)	— —	20000 (12.5)	—	—
Set, costumes, etc.	3000 (1.19)	15000 (8.57)	5000 (3.12)	15000 (4.48)	20000 (4.50)
Instruments	15000 (5.97)	15000 (8.57)	20000 (12.5)	15000 (4.48)	20000 (4.50)
Rehearsal	140000 (55.77)	30000 (17.14)	40000 (25.0)	100000 (29.87)	126000 (28.37)
Rent	15000 (5.97)	15000 (8.57)	— —	25000 (7.46)	35000 (7.88)
Miscellaneous	18000 (7.17)	30000 (17.14)	20000 (12.5)	40000 (11.96)	50000 (11.26)
Total	251000	175000	160000	334700	444000

Notes: 1. Figures in the bracket indicate the percentage of each item of cost.
2. The figures give the cost of staging the drama for a single day.
3. While drama A and B belong to the amateur, C to the experimental and D and E to the commercial categories of drama.

of actors appeared in each story, the cost of training, the difference in the make up materials, the variations in the quality of costumes etc.

While story accounted for 13.51 per cent in the case of drama E, a commercial drama, it accounted respectively at 9.96 per cent in A, 11.42 per cent in B, 11.95 per cent in D and nil in C, an experimental drama. The cost on cast did not form an important item in any of the cases under reference though the actors comprising the leading male and female characters and a large number of supporting characters constituted a numerically large segment. In drama A, B and C cast was not at all an item in the cost. Actors would have been rendering their service, as a pure honorary work, on account of their inherent interest in an artistic calling. The cost on cast was very low even in the commercial dramas.

While in D, it accounted for 4.39 per cent of the total, it accounted for 3.15 per cent in E respectively. Artistic interest would have been one reason for the low ratio of remuneration. It would also be due to the weak bargaining power of the actors in the art labour market for drama. Excepting in A, music accounted for roughly 10 per cent of the total cost in all the cases. Cost on music is stated to be high as it included costs for hiring musical instruments and recording the music. Apparently, music is an item in which technology comes to the aid in live drama. One important item in the cost was for rehearsal. It accounted for 55 per cent in A, 20.87 per cent in D, 28.57 per cent in E, 25 per cent in C and 17 per cent in B respectively. The cost for rehearsal is an indicator of the importance of training each member of the the troupe with various paraphernalia relating to the story before staging the performance in front of the audience. Another major item of cost was direction. It accounted for 18.75 per cent in C, more than 11 per cent in B, D, and E, and 7.96 per cent in A respectively. Dancers also received moderate level of remuneration in all cases. While make up man received 12.5 per cent in C and 1.99 per cent in A, it did not figure as a separate element of cost in other cases. All these items of cost fall, within the category of artistic inputs. They accounted for 77.9 per cent in A, 57.11 per cent in B, 71.87 per cent in in C, 70.59 per cent in D and 73.91 per cent in E respectively. Approximately, three fourth of the cost of production was appropriated by artistic inputs of one kind or other in all cases except in B. Part of the cost on music is towards the hire charges of various equipments comprising material input.

The rest of the cost was incurred on material inputs. Among them cost of sets, instruments, rent for the building and miscellaneous items of expenditure form the important components. Miscellaneous cost includes ordinary labour cost on various items. Roughly one quarter of the expenditure was on pure material inputs. Among the material inputs, rent for the theatre is fairly high throughout the world. Fortunately, it was not high in the case of dramas examined in the study. Significntly, the cost on rent was nil in the case of experimental drama C. In order to save rent, experimental dramas as well as many amateur performances are staged in the open ground. Apparently, most of the performances were staged in theatres with moderate facilities. Simalarly, cost can be fairly high especially for historical plays requiruing costly make-up materials and costumes. It varied from 1.19 in the case of drama A to 5.71 in the case of of drama B. Thus any drama is a joint product of creative activities of artists and humdrum inputs. It goes without saying that any drama is a costly one, which cannot be staged without recouping the cost.

Compared to the present condition the cost of staging a drama was pretty low during 1980s. A dialogue drama in Bombay or Calcutta demanding one set was stated to cost between Rs. 15000 and Rs. 30000. In Calcutta's commercial theatre a play requiring costumes of historical period has been incurring between Rs. 1200,000 and Rs. 1600,000 as cost. However, an amateur drama would have cost anywhere between Rs. 3000 to Rs. 50000 or as much as Rs. 40000 in some exceptional cases. One of Calcutta's amateur group estimated that costs of new productions would be between Rs. 15,000 and Rs. 20.000[14]. Such wide variation occurs because of the type of make up materials used, the amount paid to actors etc.

Apparently, drama becomes more of an economic activity requiring high cost of production. There is an escalation in the cost during recent years. In this context, it is worth quoting the various components of the cost involved during 1960s in the performance of *Chavittunatakam*, a dramatic genre, popular among the Latin Christians of Kerala: "The major expenditure of the troupe is the rent for the equipment, costumes, orchestra, and stage setting. Sometimes they stage the performance in a theatre, and then they have to pay the rent. Actors do not get any kind of remuneration from the troupe as in other artistic performances. Thus this art form was going on a very shaky financial foundation. There have been several occasions when troupes had to be dissolved due to dire financial strains" (see Table 5.2)

Organisational arrangements of Chavittunatakam were made in such a way that some of the firms are not keen on profit. Such firms fall within the category of pure artistic concerns of Throsby. Needless to say, they were able to stage the performances at very low cost. Chundal adds the following observation on the modus operandi of Chavittunatakam: "Chavittunatakam troupes get performances once or twice a year.

Table 5.2: Itemwise Details of Expenditure for the Staging of a Typical Chavittunatakam

i.	Rent for Costumes	Rs. 350-500
ii.	Make-up (including the materials-colour powder, paste, wig, gum etc	Rs. 300-500
iii.	Orchestra (three persons)	Rs. 200-400
iv.	Remuneration to Actor	Rs. 30
v.	Remuneration to Asan	Rs. 50
vi.	Female Actress	Rs. 150

Source: *Christian Theatre in India* (1984, St. Joseph's I.S. Press Thrissur, pp. 184-85[15].

Generally no profit is expected from the performances. The members of the troupe find other employment for their livelihood. These troupes do not get financial support from any quarter. Sometimes the organisers of the performance collect donations to meet a portion of the expenditure. In the ordinary course, the members of the troupe themselves share the whole amount of the expenditure."[16]. However, they may require a return for meeting various kinds of expenditure and for continuing the production. On the other hand, most of the other dramatic firms in the state operate for getting a profit. Commercial considerations rule the roost in such cases.

Since the cost is so high, staging of any drama cannot be carried on without financial support. In the past, as stated earlier, temples used to meet the expenses of ritual performances. During recent years, programmes have been curtailed on account of the escalation in the cost coupled with the absence of patrons willing to meet the cost. The people with money also used to patronise drama in the past. Since the 17th century, market became the main source for raising finances for any artistic activity in theWest. Entry of the market as the source for finance has been responsible for the growth of theatres on commercial lines. In turn, financing was invariably met by raising money through sale of tickets for each show. Charges varied from theatre to theatre and also on the basis of gradation of seating in the theatre. Thus with commercialism in drama, theatres became a lucrative business in many parts of the world. As seen earlier, modern theatres began to appear in India since the middle of ninenth century as a commercial venture by selling tickets for each show. In Calcutta, a top priced ticket costs about Rs. 15 in Star theatres during the seventies of the 20th century[17]. Varying rates were charged for tickets in Kerala also in the past. However, with the erosion of the popularity of theatres in the wake of the emergence of mediated drama, most of the troupes have abandoned the ticket system. Instead, what they do is to keep a bucket for collection on a voluntary basis. Another method is to raise money by printing a souvenir, containing the programmes of the troupe, list of a few interesting articles and some advertisements etc.

Dramatic Output or Returns

Output stands as a key concept in Economics. It can be in the form of physical output or mere money value. Being a service activity there is no physical output in the strict sense in the case of a drama. The statement of Anna Burger "that the property of services–or rather their result does not take an independent physical form that could be separated in time and space from the process itself" squarely holds good in the case of dramatic performance[18]. As in the case of any other service, the activities of staging a drama and its utilisation have to take place simultaneously. They are so to say "experience goods" as Caves terms them. Apparently, if it is not utilised, or consumed, by seeing it at the time of presentation, the question of output does not arise at all. Naturally, output can be evaluated only in terms of the amount spent by the consumers for utilising the performance. Variations in output take place apparently on account of variations in quality. Quality itself can be known only after the audience have utilised the product. How much money the consumers spend for seeing the drama, or for practical purpose, the mere quantum of turnover has to be reckoned as output in the case of cultural services. Output in the form of turnover becomes crucially important for the sustenance of a cultural service like drama as it requires a fairly good amount of money for its staging. While artistic drama looks upon the turnover as the source of finance for its sustenance, commercial drama regards turn over as the source for profit.

During the survey, information on the financial performance of a few dramatic troupes was gathered, while collecting data on costs and returns. Theatrical troupes regard the performance of a particular dramatic performance continuously for a number of days with the same band of artists as one performance for their accounting purpose, though in reality they are different performances. Table 5.3 gives the retuns of a few dramas.

As can be seen in the Table, there was considerable level of variations in the volume of turn over among the different dramas in the sample. Variatons occur, as stated earlier, mainly on account of quality. While the turnover of amateur drama A, was only Rs. 86000, the cost of production

Table 5.3: Cost and Returns of a Few Dramatic Performances (in Rupees)

Name of Drama	*Total Cost*	*Returns*	*Profit/Loss*	*No. of Performances*	*Profit per Performance*
1 (drama A)	251000	86000	–165000	22	–7500
2 (drama B)	175000	300000	125000	36	3472
3 (drama C)	160000	370000	210000	8	26250
4 (drama D)	2777000	3780000	1003000	210	4776
5 (drama E)	3758000	4760000	1002000	238	4210

Note: The total cost as given in Table 6.3 is higher than figures given in Table 6.1, because the cost of performing the drama per day only is shown in Table 6.1, while Table 6.3 gives the total at the end of the continuous performance of a drama for a number of days.

was Rs. 251000. There was thus a net loss of Rs. 165000. However, it managed to cover the loss, by receiving subsidy from different sources. On the other hand, B another amateur drama was able to fetch a profit of Rs. 125000 and C, an experimental drama was able to get a profit of Rs. 210000. These two dramas were not paying any salary to the actors. A major reason for getting the profit appears to be the non payment of salary to the artists who render the service on a pure honorary basis. At the same time, they were getting subsidy and aid from various sources in and above the profit.

The position of commercial dramas was altogether differet. While the turn over was as high as Rs. 47.6 lakh in the case of drama E, it was Rs. 37.8 lakh in the case of drama D. Similarly, drama D could make a gross profit of Rs. 1003000 and E, Rs. 1002000. However, if the average level of profit for each day's performance is taken, the volume of profit does not appear to be so big. It was respectively, Rs. 4776 for D, and Rs. 4210 for E, per performance. Similarly both the dramas could earn a profit because of the continuous performance for a number of days by which the fixed cost for training, script, make up materials and cost of costumes could be distributed. On an average drama D could make only a turn over Rs. 18000 per day and Drama E Rs. 20000 per day. While continuing the performance, the troupe was required to pay only the remuneration to the actors and a minimum amount of labour charges as recurring cost. Profit formed 36.1 per cent of the turnover in the case of D and 26.6 per cent in the case of E respectively. Gross profit seems to have stemmed mainly because of the low level of remuneration paid to the actors. According to well informed sources, there are many instances where the professional dramas fail to meet both ends. According to them, many of them do not earn even Rs. 2000 on an average per performance.

In the past the main source of revenue was by selling the tickets. Selling of the tickets has given way to a system known as bag collection. Amateur theatres and experimental theatres manage to survive with the subsidies or support from some local patrons. However, there has been a significant fall in the number of performances staged by all cateories of theatres during recent years.

Conclusion

Any dramatic performance is a costly business as it calls for different inputs. Dramas can hold on if they are able to secure a good return. However, the volume of return, very often does not match with the cost.

Such a situation seems to have emerged with the appearance of cinema and television as alternative sources of entertainment. They could erode the popularity of drama particularly of commercial category by skilfully utilising the technological devices in such a way as to attract the audience. In the wake of such new developments, most of the theatres running on commercial lines have disappeared. However, some of the amateur theatres and experimental theatres manage to survive not with the size of the doles collected from the audience, but from the doles the public authorities and charitable institutions render.

NOTES AND REFERENCES

1. Caves, Richard E. (2003); "Contract between art and commerce" in *Journal of Economic Perspective*, Vol. 17 No. 2 Spring 2003.
2. Caves, Richard. E. (2000); *Creative Industries: Contract between Art and Commerce* (Harvard University Press) p. 38.
3. Hamilton, Clayton (2004); *The Theory of Theatre, and Other Principles of Dramatic Criticism* (Project Gutenburg) p. 46.
4. Hamilton, Clayton (2004); *op. cit.,* p. 46.
5. Throsby, David (2001); *Economics and Culture* (Cambridge University Press) p. 97.
6. Throsby, David (2001); *op. cit.*, pp. 94-101.
7. Throsby, David (2001); *op. cit.*, p. 99.
8. Throsby, David (2001); *op. cit.*, p. 101.
9. Farley, P. Richmond (ed.) (1993); *Indian Theatre: Traditions of Performance* (New Delhi, Motilal Banrsidass Publishers Pvt. Ltd.) p. 391.
10. Farley, P. Richmond (1993); *op. cit.*, p. 394.
11. Allen, John (1973); "The Effects of subsidy on Western European Theatre in the 1970s" in Redmond James (eds.) (1973); *Drama and Society* (Cambridge University Press) p. 232.
12. Farley, P. Richmond (1993); *op. cit.*, p. 394.
13. Choondal, Chummar (1984); *Christian Theatre in India* (Thrissur, St. Thomas, I.S. Press) pp. 183-4.
14. Richmond, Farley, P. (1993); *op. cit.,* p. 429.
15. Choondal, Chummar (1984); *op. cit.,* pp. 184-85.
16. Choondal, Chummar (1984); *op. cit.,* p. 184.
17. Richmond, Farley. P. (1973); *op. cit.*, p. 433.
18. Burger, Anna (1970); *Economic Problems of Consumer Services* (Budapest, Akademiai Kiado) p. 24.

6

Career of Artists in Different Forms of Drama

As seen in the earlier Chapters, drama is a joint product of different categories of artists like the writer, the director, the actor, the musician, the dancer, and the make-up men. Similarly, drama has undergone a sea change over the years. Among the changes, the latest and perhaps the most significant one, is the emergence of the technologically mediated drama. However, in the making of all forms of drama, the contribution of artists is of paramount importance. It is they who provide the creative input to drama per se. In this chapter, a comparative picture of the functions and career of the artists, particularly that of the actors of theatrical and mediated varieties of drama is delineated by drawing empirical evidences from the dramatic scene in Malayalam.

Different Categories of Artists and Their Role in Dramatic Performance

Artists of different categories are constantly engaged in various artistic activities. They can be broadly divided into two different categories, viz., creative artists and performing artists. Poets, novelists, playwrights, painters, sculptors directors, composers, lyrists, choreographers etc., fall within the category of creative artists. Performing artists are composed of actors, dancers, musicians, puppeters and circus performers. This classification is not exclusive as performers also engage as playwrights, as Shakespeare served as a playwright as well as an actor. Artists of these two groups function in different ways with the creative group invariably operating independently, while performers often find themselves as employees of some organisation. In some cases, creative artists who are hired as playwrights are employed by dramatic troupes, or film companies.

The artists who engage in dramatic activities differ very much in the gradation of their services. It was playwrights who had a premiere role in any drama for a long period. Any drama can be stated to be the enactment of a text written by a playwright. Some of the writers are highly gifted authors. Furthermore, in the past drama was noted for the literary qualities of the text. The playwrights like Shakespeare, or Moliere, became renowned artists for creating classical texts. Their works could be enjoyed as works for their literary qualities. With the emergence of the mediated drama, there has been an erosion in the dominant position of the writer. Very often, they are compelled to compromise their position. At the same time, many of the talented young writers are tempted to seek their fortune in writing scripts for films and television. In so doing, very often they are transformed themselves as mere employees of the the producing concerns. In close succession, directors have gained importance invariably at the expense of writers. The director himself may be combining different functions. While some of them might be playwrights, some others serve as mere senior actors. Very often, directors guide and control the dramatic troupe without which no drama can be staged. In this connection, what Richmond Farley states about amateur theatres squarely holds good in the case of all kinds of drama. He states that "the very life of a group may be in the hands of one individual who brings a sense of unity and purpose to the activities of the group"[1].

With the appearance of cinema, film directors seem to have acquired further importance in their stature as artists, a position somewhat similar to that of the writers and painters. In the opinion of Stam, the director, "is no longer merely the servant of a pre-existing text, novel, screen play but a creative artist in his own/her own right"[2]. Some authors maintain that cinema itself has to be reckoned as another form of art, "the seventh art", which has has become a new mode of expression, analogous to painting or novel. Such a line of thinking has paved the way for the emergence of a new concept known as auteurism, which looks upon the director as the main artist in a film[3]. Whether auterism as such is tenable, for explaining the key role of the director, the emerging situation projects the rise of the director as the crucial figure at least in the case of the mediated drama like cinema. In the opinion of Gary Williams, the mission of the director in the past was to function as a kind "of surrogate for the playwright". Since late 1960s, the idea of the director as the primary artist, or at least as a kind of co- equal with the playwright was emerging. Such a change seems to have become strong with the emergence of mediated drama in which he acquired predominant status relegating the playwright, to an an insignificant rank[4]. In fact, it is the director who structures the story through editing after shooting the scenes in different locations on varying occasions.

A host of artists comprising the actors, musicians, dancers etc., are in the fray in the staging of a drama. Nevertheless, it is the actor who plays the key role in any theatrical drama. As Martin Esslin puts it, "the artist who performs the mimetic action, the actor thus stands at the very centre of the art of drama"[5]. Actors appear as leading characters and supporting characters. In the opinion of William Gary, while acting, actors use their body as performance instrument, and their own lives as subjects[6]. In doing so, their body is being commodified as some sort of item suitable for sale. As another authority enjoins, "the star is a total item of merchandise, there is not an inch of her body, not a shred of her soul, not a memory of her life that cannot be thrown in the market"[7]. At the same time, it is through their acting skill, fictional elements acquire the semblance of reality. The problem which the actor faces is to transform the fiction of the play into artistic stage reality. The creative actor according to Stanislavsky is, "completely carried away by the play in which he is appearing for it is only then that he can enter fully into the feeling of his part without being aware of his own feeling"[8]. In other words, he totally identifies with the character. Zerilli adds further and maintains that what the actor does, "is creating signs [images] as well as entering those images /actions with an appropriate degree of psychological engagement of voice/body/ mind to capture, engage and direct the audiences' attention of"[9]. In the past, audience used to sit very close to actors and occasionally made certain comments during the performance. However, of late, actors could manage to remove the spectators from the stage and elevate their stature further[10]. The actor is an iconic sign par excellence, a real human being, who has become a sign for human being[11]. In the opinion of Esslar, it is the tension between the real actor on the one hand, and the functional character as as an iconic sign on the other, that creates one of the main attractions of drama[12]. According to him three stages are discernible in the acting. As he puts, "an actor appearing on the stage or the screen is, in the first place, himself the real person—with his physical characters, his voice and temperament—secondly, himself transformed, disguised by costumes, make up, an assumed voice, a mental attitude—with fictional character he is playing—the stage figure, thirdly and most importantly, there is the fiction itself, for which he stands and which ultimately, will emerge in the mind of the individual spectator watching the play or film"[13]. Acting becomes a creative activity resulting in an interpretation of the world in new ways through sound or body expression or gesture of the actor.

Behaviour of the Artist in the Labour Market

Actors who perform mimetic action require material means for their sustenance. For this purpose, they sell their artistic skill like other workers in exchange for rewards. They may also demand better facilities like other members of society. A behavioural pattern similar to that of other labour, though not to the same degree, is likely to persist in the calculus of actors also. However, as Throsby states, "artistic labour markets present some intriguing challenges to a labour economist seeking to understand the standard variables usually considered to models of labour market behaviour, labour supply, wage determination, earning distribution, career paths and so on"[14]. In the case of artistic activity like drama, cooperative effort of both artists and non-artists is required, costume makers and make-up men also render some sort of artistic input. The distinction between art and non-art labour is an issue which has not been clearly demarcated. At the same time, artists as a whole are not a homogeneous class. Naturally all of them cannot be clubbed as one class. An equally important issue is what should be the the norms under which remuneration is to be paid. Productivity which is recognised as the main yardstick for determining wages has not recorded any improvement in the case of artists for a long period. Ipso facto, productivity per se cannot be counted as a criterion for the payment of remuneration for artists. However, with rise in wages in other sectors of employment as a result of rise in productivity would have adverse impact on the supply of artists in drama.

Apparently, the norms under which remuneration is to be paid to actors have become a bane of contention among the authors especially because there is an oversupply of artists leading to a situation of starving artists. According to some authors, artists are unmindful about monetary rewards. As Esslin adds, "a deep need for self expression, an imperious creative urge, inspires many of the creative artists–writers, actors, directors designers-involved in the drama is beyond doubt. They are invariably pleased with the process of creation rather than outcome of the work"[15]. In other words, most of them seem to be content with psychic satisfaction.

Nevertheless, such a line of thinking cannot be taken as valid under all circumstances. At least some actors would be interested to get better remuneration. In support of such a contention, Esslin himself quotes the parody:

> If our spot had gone forward we had all been made men
> O sweet bathy Bottom/Thus hath we lost six pence a day

He adds, "financial gain is not the only motivation for dramatic performance, although in our own time it is the principal one"[16]. Toeing to the line of thinking of Frey, Towse, a noted authority on cultural economics, enjoins that "as with motivation, reward can be either intrinsic emphasising psychic satisfaction from peer recognition, enhanced reputation and so on, or extrinsic in the form of money. Fery's theory is that, unless intrinsic motivation is met with intrinsic reward, there will be 'crowding out'; incentive and reward must be matched.—an artist who is driven by inner motivation is not only not stimulated to produce work by monetary reward, he or she should even be demotivated by it"[17]. Incentive and reward must be matched. Taking a slightly different stand, Stanislavsky, the noted actor, succinctly explains the matter in the case of a creative artist thus: "there can be no question of sacrificing everything for his art, for all creative work is a series of life affirming situation. –It is impossible to reach the peaks of creative genius by saying to oneself 'I renounce life, I give up its beauty, its joys and pleasures because this act of renunciation of mine is the sacrifice I make for all mankind'.—The opposite is true. There can be no question of sacrifice in art. In it, everything is fascinating, every thing is interesting, every thing absorbs the mind. Everything in life exerts a tremendous attraction on the artist". His concludes that "no artist can exist if he is expected to renounce life like a monk"[18]. Johnson another literary luminary enjoins 'for we that give pleasure must please to live'[19]. Apparently, actors must be sufficiently rewarded, which need not necessarily be in terms of money, if at all they are to be able and willing to remain in the field and strive to please people.

However, there is wide variation in the rate of remuneration between the artists of the ordinary drama and technologically mediated drama. What can be the reason for such wide variation in the remuneration of the two categories of actors? Furthermore, the super stars get abnormally high rate of remuneration when an ordinary actor gets only a meagre amount of salary. How the phenomenon of super stars has emerged when the majority of actors remain as 'a starving class' poses a question requiring an answer. Such anomalous conditions seem to have stemmed from the economies of scale achieved by mediated drama both in production and marketing. Dramatic theatres are by no means capable of achieving economies of scale even if they operate on commercial lines. Needless to say, mediated drama is sure to have powerful impact on the supply and behavioural pattern of actors. Apparently, the talented artists desert drama and move to the technologically mediated drama. Evidently, drama may find it difficult to hold on in the face of the depletion of the supply of talented actors.

A field study was made to uncover various facets, relating to the career and behavioural pattern of the artists by collecting empirical evidences from a few Malayalam theatres and Malayalam tele-serials. The study was designed to draw a comparative picture of the career paths of the actors, both in drama proper, and mediated drama represented by tele-serials. Data on the demographic details, socio-economic profile, the monetary rewards to both classes of actors, their order of preferences on the different forms of drama etc., were gathered by interviewing both the categories of actors with the help of open ended schedules. Altogether 131 dramatic actors and 50 serial actors were interviewed. As a starting point, a few directors were also interviewed with structured schedules. The length of service as director and the rate of remuneration received by each one were ascertained.

Stature of Dramatic Directors

The number of dramas directed by each one can shed light on the standing of theatrical dramatic directors.

Table 6.1: Number of Dramas Directed by Each Director

Range of Dramas Directed	*No. of Directors*
1 - 5	2
6 - 10	4
11 - 15	4
16 - 30	4
31 and above	5
Total	20

As to be inferred from the Table, most of the directors had sufficient experience in directing dramas. Those who directed only less than 5 dramas numbered only 2 and those with 6-10 were only 4. The number of directors with more than 10 dramas were 14 which formed 70 per cent of the total. Apparently, they were veteran directors with sufficient standing in the dramatic field.

Though monetary consideration as such does not constitute the main motive for any artistic activity, money also counts much for the various reasons as indicated earlier in the Chapter. Artists as such are not an exception. Table 6.2 gives the level of earning of the dramatic directors.

Directors as a whole were not getting any fabulous amount as remuneration for directing drama. Those who were getting more than Rs. 1000 as remuneration were only 6 in numbers. In percentage terms, it formed 30. According to the current standards, an amount of Rs. 1000 is

Table 6.2: Range of Remuneration to the Directors

Range of Remuneration	*No. of Directors*
Nil remuneration	5
Remuneration at less than Rs. 1000	3
Remuneration at Rs. 1000	6
Remuneration of more than Rs. 1000	6
Total	20

only a meagre amount particularly when direction of a drama requires many days of preparation. At the same time, as many as five directors were not receiving any remuneration at all. They were directing the dramas on purely voluntary basis. The rest of the respondents forming 45 per cent of the sample were getting only Rs. 1000 or less as remuneration. Apparently, directing a drama was not at all a lucrative career. Most of them seemed to have ventured in the field purely on account of their keen interest in artistic activities. Some of them were in fact, financing drama from their own pocket. It follows that the dedication and willingness of many directors to continue in the field without bothering about the remuneration counts much in the survival of drama.

If it were so, why did they enter the field? One typical director indicated that he continues in drama though it brings financial losses to him, because of his keen interest in drama as an important cultural endeavour. Another director, confided that he looked upon drama from an artistic angle and not from pecuniary consideration. Though there is keen competition from mediated forms of drama, dramas thrive because of the dedication to it, exhibited by many directors. One director was emphatic that one can succeed in dramatic career only if there is dedication to it, especially because of the heavy responsibility to organise and manage the affairs of a dramatic troupe. They have not only to organise the troupe but also to manage and run the affairs very carefully. In fact, the success of any troupe depends on the skill of the director. Saithan Joseph, an eminent director succinctly describes the position thus: "The management of a dramatic club is as difficult as to ferry a jackal, cock, and paddy in the same boat at the same time. Artists in a troupe are composed of people with contrasting characteristics. A troupe can be managed skilfully by meeting the requirements of different artists. Otherwise the club will crumble"[20].

Profile and Career of Actors

Actors, the most important human input in a drama, assume, as stated earlier, the image of characters depicted in a story. Talented persons, who are capable of hiding their own personality and displaying the qualities of characters, only can succeed as actors. Nevertheless, labour issues, many of them complex in nature, have to be uncovered for understanding the role and functions of actors. Data on those various aspects relating to the actors and serial actors were collected during the field study. What follows is an attempt to uncover the issues on the basis of the findings of the field study.

As as a starting point, demographic characteristics of the dramatic actors relating to sex, education, age etc., were delineated. (*see* Table 6.3)

Table 6.3: Agewise Distribution of Actors in Malayalam Drama (%)

Age	*Males*	*Females*	*Average of the Two*
15-25	—	—	—
26-25	15.85	14.28	15.26
36-45	47.50	44.89	46.56
46-55	32.92	24.48	29.77
56 and above	3.65	16.32	8.65
Total	100	100	100

As can be seen in the Table, young artists below the age of 25 were totally nil in the list. Approximately, 15 per cent of the actors of box sexes fall withn the age group 26-35. On the other hand, nearly half the actors were in the age group 36-45. Those between 46 to 55 formed the second largest category. Those above 56 years and above formed 8.65 per cent. Youngsters would normally constitute the largest group among tha actors. They used to flock to the dramatic field even if remuneration is very low. Many of them will start acting at a young age as a stepping up process for advancing their career. Instead, the middle aged group formed the largest contingent among them. Nevertheless, it corresponds to the average mean age of actors in Australia. The average age group of artists in Australia was about 46 years according to a study[21]. Citing the same Towse states that "on an average artists tend to be older than the general workforce or the total population"[22]. Though the prime age group in the case of females usually comprises below 25 years, there was no female artist below 25 years. Apparently youngsters are lukewarm to enter dramatic career. Apparently, those who entered the dramatic field nearly 15 to 20 years back alone are the people who dominate dramatic scene. One probable reason for the domination of the seniors in combination with the absence of youngsters would be the growth of cinema and television. Such mediated drama would be offering alternative opportunities to artists with better remuneration and glamour. Table 6.4 which gives the agewise details of Malayalam serial actors will shed more light in the matter.

Table 6.4: Agewise Classification of the Serial Actors (%)

Age group	*Males*	*Females*	*Average of the Two*
15-25	7.4	21.0	15.0
26-35	—	3.01	1.66
36-45	44.44	12.10	26.66
46-55	22.22	33.32	28.33
55 and above	25.91	30.29	28.33
Total	100	100	100

As can be seen in the Table, youngsters below 25 years formed roughly 15 per cent. This is in contrast to the absence of any dramatic actor below 25 years. Those who were well above 36 accounted for the bulk of the respondents. It could be ascertained that serials began to appear in Malayalam only from 1990s when TV was thrown open to private sector. With the entry of the private sector, more and more serials were presented leading to increased demand for actors. The serial actors who began to surface since then, seemed to be holding on by creating a niche for themselves, without leaving any space to the youngsters. Most of the actors who stepped into serials were actors of drama on whom further reference will be made in another section.

Educational Profile of the Actors

Education also counts much in the career of any class of people. Artists cannot be an exception to this general pattern. Table 6.5, gives the classification of artists on the basis of educational profile.

Table 6.5: Educational Profile of the Dramatic Actors (%)

Level of Education	*Men*	*Women*	*Average of the Two*
Below SSSLC	4.99	8.16	6.01
SSLC	41.46	46.96	43.51
Pre Degree	41.46	42.85	41.98
Degree	9.75	2.04	6.87
P.G	2.43	—	1.52
Total	100	100	100

As can be seen, the overwhelming majority of the respondents had an education upto SSLC or Pre-degree. Though degree holders were very few among the actors, the number of degree students in the state exceeds well over 1.65 lakh. Apparently, educational qualification does not count much in the career of the artists. The educated would have preferred other occupations with better opportunities than to stick on to drama which offers only meagre sums of money as remuneration. After all, what is required for acting consists of qualities which encompass gestures of the face and hands in combination with the ability to embody moods and convey meanings in the dramatic context. People who are endowed with such skills flock into the acting career which does not require much of an educational qualification.

Table 6.6: Educational Profile of the Serial Actors (%)

Level of Education	*Men*	*Women*	*Average of the Two*
Below SSSLC	3.70	6.60	5.00
SSLC	18.51	30.30	25.00
Pre Degree	29.62	33.30	31.66
Degree	33.33	24.24	28.33
P.G	14.81	6.06	10.00
Total	100	100	100

As to be inferred from the Table, serial actors were better educated in comparison with dramatic actors. With 31 per cent, pre-degree holders formed the largest group. Among them females formed 33 per cent against 27 per cent among the males. On the other hand, with more than 33 per cent, males formed the largest group among graduates. On the whole degree holders accounted for 28.33 per cent. Post graduates among the males formed 18.81 per cent against 6 per cent among the females. Better monetary rewards and glamour would have attracted the educated to a career in serial acting.

The standing of actors in the dramatic field can be known from the number of dramas in which each one has acted. Table 6.7 indicates the number of dramas acted by the actors.

As to be inferred from the Table, all the actors seem to be veterans by acting in a large number of dramas. Those who acted in the range of 1-5, formed nil. On the other hand, those who acted in 6-10 dramas formed 12.27 per cent and those in the range 11-15 accounted for 8.95 per cent. Those in the range 15-20 formed 11.85 Those who acted in the range 21-

Table 6.7: Number of Dramas Acted by Each Dramatic Actors (%)

No. of Dramas in which Acted	*Males*	*Females*	*Average of the Two*
1-5		—	—
6-10	7.31	20.40	12.27
11-15	3.65	14.28	8.96
16-20	7.31	16.32	11.85
21-25	4.87	8.16	6.51
26-30	0.04	2.24	1.12
Above 30	76.82	38.77	57.79
Total	100	100	100

30 formed 7.63 per cent-The remaining respondents accounting for nearly 57,79 percent, acted in more than 30 dramas. Among them males accounted for 76.82 per cent and females 38.77 per cent respectively. Apparently, they are veterans who stood thick and thin in the field of drama.

Table 6.8: Number of Serials Acted by Each Serial Actor (%)

Range of Serials	*Males*	*Females*	*Average of the Two*
1-20 episodes	14.81	27.27	21.66
21-50	25.92	29.39	33.37
51-100	33.33	21.21	26.66
101-150	14.81	9.09	11.66
151-200	7.41	3.03	5.00
Not known	3.7	—	1.66
Total	100	100	100

In the case of serials as a whole, each episode lasts for a number of days. The length of acting career can be known by ascertaining the number of episodes in which each actor has acted as the criterion. Most of them had a long period of acting career; those who acted in less than 20 episodes numbered only 21.66 per cent. While 33.37 per cent acted in between 21-50 episodes and those between 51 to 100 formed 26.66 per cent. While 11.66 per cent acted in the range 101-150 and 5 per cent above 151 episodes. Evidently the majority of the actors were veteran acting in large number of serials.

There is a belief that artists engage in artistic career without bothering about monetary consideration. However, in the wake of material prosperity, they may also opt for higher rates of remuneration in order to seek a comfortale living. What exactly is the position of dramatic artists? (*see* Table 6.9).

Table 6.9: Rate of Remuneration of the Dramatic Actors (%)

Level of Remuneration per Performance	*Male Actors*	*Female Actors*	*Average of the Two*
Below Rs. 500	3.65	4.08	3.81
Bet- Rs. 501-600	19.51	14.28	17.55
Bet-Rs. 601- 700	40.24	16.32	31.29
Bet-Rs. 701-800	28.04	59.15	39.96
Above Rs 800	8.53	6.12	7.63
Total	100	100	100

As can be seen in the Table, all the actors were getting only meagre sums of money. The average rate of remuneration per performance works out to Rs. 629 only. A day's performance can be staged after so many days of rehearsal. Evidently, career of an actor in drama cannot be regarded as a lucrative one. While those who were getting a remuneration in the range of Rs. 600-700 formed 31 per cent and those in the range Rs. 701-800 were 40 per cent of the whole. Significantly, while ladies in the range of Rs. 701-800 formed 59 per cent, males formed only 28 per cent. An amount of Rs. 700 forms only a meagre sum according to the current standards. Those who were getting more than Rs. 800 formed only 7.63 per cent of the total. There were well over 20 per cent of the actors who were getting less than Rs. 600 as remuneration. Apparently, most of them fall within the category of starving artists. In other countries also artists get less amounts of reuneration. As Towse adds "artists earn less than other workers when age and schooling are standardised"[22]. As remuneration is very low, many of them opt for alternative occupations. Some of them are supported by the members of the family.

While actors of drama were getting only a meagre amount as remuneration, serial actors in television were getting fairly attractive rate of remuneration. Table 6.10 gives the range of earnings of serial actors in Malayalam serials.

The remuneration received by serial actors was much higher than that of the dramatic actors. The level of remuneration of all the serial actors was well over Rs. 1000. At the same time, none of the actors in drama received Rs. 1000 as remuneration. The average rate of remuneration per episode works out at Rs. 4866 in the case of serial actors. As mentioned earlier, it was only Rs. 629 in the case of actors in drama. Apparently, the average rate of remuneration of a serial actor was nearly eight times higher than that of an actor in a drama. Unlike the rest of India, where some of the super stars in television earn more than Rs. one

Table 6.10: Range of Remuneration of the Serial Actors

Range of Remuneration	*Males*	*Female*	*Average of the Two*
Rs. 1000-1999	—	6.06	3.33
2000-3000	22.22	3.03	11.66
3000 3999	11.11	18.18	15.00
4000-5000	37.03	15.15	25.00
5000 5999	14.81	42.42	30.00
6000 and more	14.81	1.15	15.00
	100	100	100

lakh per day's performance, there seems to be no super stars in Malayalam. Among the respondents, only one actor was getting Rs. 10000 and another Rs. 8000 for a single day's performance. Apparently, Stanislavsky's stance, on which reference was made earlier holds good in the case of serial actors in so far as remuneration is concerned. Similarly, the observation of Esslar about playwrights of Britain that "publicly financed media of radio and television continues to provide a means for playwrights to earn a decent living without selling out completely" seems to be the pattern in the case of serial actors[24]. On the other hand, dramatic actors are invariably compelled to take alternative occupations for making both ends meet. Apparently, acting was not full time career with the dramatic actors as a whole. No serial actor turned to alternative occupation. One interesting aspect was that all dramatic actors were having no experience in television acting. On the other hand, practically all serial actors started their career as dramatic actors. Once their hold in serial acting was well established, no body turned back to drama. Instead, some of them opted for cinema and thereby could earn even still higher rates of remuneration. If monetary reward for acting in drama is so low, the question is, why so many people stick to drama. In order to find an answer to the question, actors themselves were asked to explain the reasons for sticking on to drama. (see Table 6.11)

Table 6.11: Reasons for Taking up Drama as a Career

Reasons for acting in Drama	*Males*	*Females*	*Average of the Two*
Interest in acting	87.80	73.46	80.66
Absence of other occupations	12.19	16.32	14.26
Family background	—	8.16	4.08
Starting point as a career in television	—	2.04	1.02
Total	100	100	100

As can be seen, more than 80 per cent of actors entered the field because of their interest in acting. Nearly 14 per cent entered the field because of the absence of other occupations. Some of them started it as a stepping stone to television. Family background also counted as the motive with a few female actors. Since most of them were motivated with acting, they would not have bothered much about remuneration. At the same time, there is an inherent urge on the part of people to imitate others. Desire to acting seems to arise because of such an urge. Some of them were members of dramatic clubs too.

The same question was asked to serial actors. They were unanimous in stating that they embraced a career in serial acting because of their interest in acting. Some of them indicated that they were enamoured by the glamour of television. Family circumstances also induced them to take acting career in serials and cinema. Monetary reward was not mentioned as an additional reason though most of them opted for serial acting by consideration of better remuneation.

To elucidate their commitment to different forms of drama, they were asked to indicate the order of preferences as 1, 2, 3. Table 6.12 gives the preferences of actors to different forms of drama

As indicated in the Table 6.12, 78.33 per cent of the respondents expressed acting in tele-serials as their first choice. Cinema formed the first choice with 15 per cent of the respondents and drama formed the first choice wih only 3.3 per cent. Interestingly, it could be ascertained that the person who preferred drama seems to be the same person who could not gain much popularity reckoned in terms of the number of serials

Table 6.12: Order of Preference of Serial Actors for Different Forms of Drama

Category of Drama	*First Choice*	*Second Choice*	*Third Choice*
1. Tele-serials	78.33	15.0	—
2. cinema	15.00	70.0	3.33
3. drama	3.30	3.3	18.33
4. no choice	1.66	—	—
Total	100	88.3	21.66

he acted and the volume of remuneration he received. Cinema was the second choice with 70 per cent of the respondents. Very few opted drama either as a second choice or third choice. Apparently, drama has lost its attraction with practically all the serial actors. Interestingly, the vast majority of them were actors in drama. They abandoned drama once television appeared in the scene and opted for tele-serials. Though some of them cherish the idea of acting in cinema, and some of them manage to find a berth in the world of cinema, nobody is interested to act in drama. Apparently, monetary consideration counts much with most of them. When such a situation persists, chances for drama to regain its past glory cannot be rated as bright.

Nevertheless, at least a minority of actors still prefer drama. Significantly, the students of Drama School, Thrissur with whom an enquiry was made, are emphatic in their preference to drama. One of the questions asked was why they joined the school of drama? Of the 21 students, who were interviewed, 17 stated that they joined the course because of their interest in acting in live dramas as a career. On the other hand, only one student indicated that he joined the school as a stepping stone for the entry into television. The reason with the remaining three was the absence of other options. Nevertheless, all the students including those who preferred acting watched television daily because of its easy accessibility. Another question asked to them was to shed light on their future plan. For this question, 13 students favoured a career in drama. Only two students favoured a career in television. The rest numbering six had no specific plan. It shows that the majority are keen to remain in the dramatic field. Apparently, at least some actors still retain an interest in drama in spite of better opportunities in television.

Conclusion

In sum, it can be stated that a good number of stage actors cling to dramatic theatres, because of their keen artistic interest, though the remuneration is vey low. Nevertheless, some of them air for a career in teleseials. On the whole, the supply of stage actors is declining over the years as very few youngsters seem to be seeking a career in stage drama and if at all they appear in drama, it is looked upon at least by a few as a stepping stone for a brighter career in television. In this context, what Richmond Farley states about the interest of young artists holds good in the case of Malayalam actors also. He states, "despite frequent protests to the contrary, young artists see the theatre as a stepping stone to a career in films.—The dream of many young actors is to break into the Hindi film industry in Bombay—or to be hired to play in a TV serial"[25].

Some interesting observations were made by the actors, who were interviewed about the supply of actors in Kerala. One actor, observed that drama is immortal and it will remain as an art so long as human life exists. However, all of them conceded that drama is facing stiff competition from mediated drama. One reason for the declining fortune of drama stems mainly because of deterioration in the quality of drama during recent years. Some actors suggested the need for experimentation of new forms of drama as a way out to face the challenge from televisuion. Another suggestion was for making the study of drama as part of the curriculam. Another actor observed that enough committed actors are not coming forward because, many of them are not happy with the low rate of remuneration. They feel that they cannot survive with the meagre amount of income from drama. As a way out, most of them suggested the need for public support. Some of them even suggested the need for extending welfare pension to all the artists. One actor, even complained that media is ignoring them. No wonder, shortage occurs on account of the meagre amount of remuneration received by the actors coupled with the dissatisfaction of the youngsters for the traditional occupations. Instead, they seek their fortune in serials and if possible, in cinema because of the high rate of remuneration and the glamour attached to them. In other words, it is the weight of the economic factors which rules the roost in pulling down the dramatic theatres.

All the serial actors who were interviewd expressed the view that they have entered the field of acting in serials because of their keen interest in acting. Some of them expressed that they remain in the field because of the glamour. Better monetary reward would be an important factor which attracted them to the field, though nobody expressed it in clear terms, because all of them moved to television from stage drama once TV appeared in the scene and nobody went back to drama like the lone boy of Hamelin. Surprisingly, the majority of the students of the school of Drama, still prefer a career in theatrical drama, though the bargaining power of stage actors has been weakned.

Nevertheless, acting like any other art will be taken up only by those who are inspired in it by some inner calling which is unevenly distributed. Among such people, those who are endowed with superior qualities will end up as serial actors and film stars. Those who are not endowed with superior qualities may still opt for a career as actors in stage drama. They can meet local demand for performance. Survival of drama thus relies on the uneven distribution of talent among the people.

NOTES AND REFERENCES

1. Farley Richmond (1993); *Indian Theatrical Tradition of Performance* (Delhi, Banarsidas Publishers) p. 394.

2. Stam Robert (2000); *Film Theory: An Introduction,* (Blackwell Publishers Inc.) p. 83.
3. Stam Robert (2000); *op. cit.,* p. 83.
4. William Gary Jay (2010); "Director, Text, Actor and Performance in the Post Modern Period;" in Philip. B. Zarrilli *et al.* (2010); *Theatre Histories an Introduction* (New York, Routledge, Taylor, Francis Group) p. 514.
5. Esslin, Martin (1987); *The Field of Drama* (*New York, Metheun,*) pp. 25 and 28.
6. William Garry Jay (2010); *op. cit.,* p. 473.
7. Jowett Garth and Linton James. M. (1980) quotes from Morin Edgar's book (1960); *The Stars* in *Movies as Communication* (London, Sage Publications) p. 79.
8. Stanislavsky on the Art of the Stage; Translated by David Magarshack (London, Faber and Faber) p. 28.
9. Zarrilli Philip (2002); "Introduction" in *Acting Reconsidered a Theoretical and Practical Guide* (London, Routledge) p. 16.
10. McConachie, Bruce; "Theatre for Knowledge through Feeling 1700-1800" in Williams Gary Jay (ed.) (2010); *Theatre Histories: An Introduction* (New York, Rutledge Taylor & Francis) p. 243.
11. Esslin, Martin (1987); *op. cit.*, p. 56.
12. Esslin, Martin (1987); *op. cit.*, p. 59.
13. Esslin, Martin (1987); *op. cit.*, p. 58
14. Throsby, David (2001); *Economics and Culture* (Cambridge, University Press) p. 120.
15. Esslin, Martin (1987); *op. cit.*, p. 135.
16. Esslin Martin (1987); *op. cit.*, p. 133.
17. Towse Ruth (2010); *Cultural Economics* (Cambridge, University Press) p. 315.
18. Stanislavsky; *op. cit.*, p. 109.
19. Esslin Martin quotes from Johnson. See Esslin Martin (1987); *op. cit.*, p. 135.
20. Saithan Joseph in Dr. K. Sreekumar (2004); *Orumukham OruJanapriya Natakavediyud Midippukal* (Mal) p. 62.
21. Towse Ruth (2010); *op. cit.*, p. 328.
22. Towse Ruth (2010); *op. cit.*, p. 328.
23. Towse Ruth (2010); *op. cit.*, p. 330.
24. Esslin Martin (1996); "The electronic media and British Drama" in Shank Theodore *Contemporary British Theatre* (1996) (Palgrave Macmilan) p. 179.
25. Farley Richmond (1993); *op. cit.,* p. 414.

7

Significance of Audience and their Behavioural Pattern in Drama

Audience can be stated to be the persons who assemble in a place to watch a performance or to listen to a music concert or speech. In a drama, they form the third important segment. Their importance assumes added significance as any drama is performed in front of the audience. Drama itself is not a finished product till the staging is completed. The audiences themselves have to go to the theatre and to be present there for viewing the product. The significance of audience in a drama along with their behaviourl pattern is delineated in this Chapter.

Importance of Audience in Drama

As already stated, audience form one of the triumvirates in a drama. According to the classical tradition, drama becomes complete only with the presence of audience. Apparently, some sort of interaction between the artists and the audience is inherent. Their importance assumes added significance as they are supposed to recoup the funds needed for the drama. The admission fee has been the main source of funds for drama for a long period. Audience pay money for seeing a drama. The amount will be large, if they are satisfied with its quality. In turn, producers evince keen interest to produce dramas which satisfy the tastes of the audience. With the growth of TV, a new mechanism for raising funds has evolved. As seen in Chapter 5, audience does not for practical purposes pay money or pays only a minimum amount for seeing a TV programme. Instead, the advertisers or sponsors of programmes meet the charges as a device for promoting the sale of goods marketed by them. Advertisers who are interested to popularise their brands of goods, look upon a large number of audience, watching the show as an ideal time for relaying advertisements of their own goods for which they pay the bill for the programme. The larger the size of audience, the larger amount of advertisement charges the channels receive. Thus the presence of audience is of paramount importance for getting enough money.

Audience: Consumer or Partner?

In the usual economic terminology, any person who avails the service or utilises it, is termed the consumer. On his part, the consumer utilises the product till he attains maximum utility. As a consumer, he goes on purchasing a commodity till the utility he gets is equal to the price he pays. Since the consumer thus effects the purchases, the producers produce and sell commodities which are preferred by the consumers. They are eager to produce a commodity in such a way as to attract the largest number of consumers. The consumers' position is naturally to that of a sovereign who is supposed to dictate terms to the producer, though in the real world, they may not be able to exercise their sovereignty. Nevertheless, consumers' sovereignty is recognised as the axiom around which productive activities revolve.

On the other hand, drama as such is a cultural service, which has to be consumed as and when it is produced. At the same time, in the case of any cultural service or product, there is total uncertainty regarding its receptivity till it is marketed. Even if aproducer takes the maximum care, it may not meet the approval of the consumer. In the cultural services, the consumer who utilises a service is known as audience. If so, can the audience be equated to a consumer? Needless to say, there is a growing tendency among various authors to regard them as mere consumers. Nevertheless, such a tendency to equate audience with consumer does not seem to be based on sound reasons. Production of any commodity under capitalist conditions is meant for sale. However, production of arts and culture is not meant for sale like an ordinary commodity. Any cultural commodity is a creative activity through which the artist communicates the reality as he sees it. As a communication process, it is neither addressed to all, nor meant to satisfy anybody and everybody. In other words, as Fischer notes, "a work of art does not have to be understood and approved by everyone"[1]. Apparently, it is a communication addressed to an audience of the artist's choice. In so doing, he does not ask himself as Hancock poses, "how do I write this subject in such a way as to appeal to the maximum number of people?"[2] Instead, he writes to meet the interests of those who can understand and appreciate what he writes. The Indian dramatist Tendulkar clearly states the same in clear terms thus: "—Viewer has to be someone who respects my freedom to choose the subject of my drama, possesses a lively imagination, and savor artistic allusion, subtlety and naturalness, instead of well spoken inanities and showy plot-twists while watching a play"[3]. In other words, the audience should be sufficiently imaginative to understand the meaning of the play. It goes without saying that he cannot be equated with the consumer of a good, say for example a piece of cake. Furthermore, the term appreciation, rather than satisfaction is invariably used for indicating the benefits accruing from gazing at a work of art. Needless to say, appreciation is totally distinct from the term consumption as it is denoted in economics. In such a situation, the tendency to club the audience and the consumer as one class, cannot claim to be to be a sound proposition.

In fact, the audience is more than a mere consumer for other reasons as well. He is, as mentioned earlier, some sort of a partner in the very process of production of a cultural product like drama. In the past, artistic activities were performed as a collective effort. All the citizens contributed a share and attended the function. Naturally, audiences were partners in such ventures. With the emergence of capitalism, cultural activities like drama also witnessed serious changes. The appropriation of ownership of dramatic troupes by businessmen and the commercial orientation of dramatic performance were the important changes which thus ensued. The move towards commercialisation in drama also would have favoured passivity among audience. Paradoxically, the entry of technologically mediated drama has effectively halted the move of drama to pure commercialism. In fact, it is the commercial theatres and not artistic dramas that have been seriously threatened by the mediated drama. So long as drama remains as a Janus–faced cultural activity, there is a limit up to which it can be tilted towards commercialism. In other words, drama has to retain certain amount of artistic ingredient. In turn, it has to be appreciated like any cultural product.

However, very little difference between audience and consumers can be noticed in the eyes of a casual observer. Actually, audience of any drama impregnated with cultural contents are more than mere consumers. Instead, they still retain some level of of partnership in the performance of such dramas. Even the mediated drama contains ingredients of cultural contents and symbolic formats. People with sufficient experience and knowledge alone are in a position to understand and appreciate them. Naturally, audiences cannot be clubbed with consumers of regular material commodities.

At the same time, it has become a fait accompli to club audience of the mediated drama as passive and not active in understanding and appreciating them. Passive audiences are not expected to make any meaning other than the one intended by the author. On the other hand, active audiences are those who give a new meaning, sometimes differing from what is in the mind of the author. Furthermore, in a drama, as in that of any other literary work, there would be gaps. It is the prevalence of such gaps, which instigates thinking process and facilitates the ground for appreciation of art. The situation is similar to what Wolfang Iser speaks of the interaction between the text and the reader. In his words, "he is drawn into the events and made to supply, what is meant from what is not said. What is said only appears to take on a significance as a reference to what is not said, it is the implication and not the statement that gives shape and weight to the meaning"[4]. Admittedly, it is the the audience who provides meaning to works of art by filling the gap in them are those who become active. However, they should be endowed with sufficient education and maturity for understanding and appreciating such works. The cultural background of the audience naturally becomes an important factor. Audiences become active when they interpret the work by filling the gap. When they thus transform themselves as active participants, they cannot be relegated to the level of a mere consumer. Even otherwise, attitudes and beliefs of audiences will have a bearing on interpreting the meaning of the messages of the products. As Abercrombie enjoins, "audiences are not blank sheets of paper on which media messages can be written; members of an audience will have prior attitudes and beliefs which will determine how effective media messages are"[5]. Even audiences of soaps would be endowed with sufficient capacity to understand and appreciate the behaviour of characters and the inner meanings of the plot, As Bielby puts, "they feel that they know the narrative and its qualities better than the producers do" apparently on account of their long acquaintance with the narrative content and structure of the soaps. As he adds further, "because soap opera narratives and characters are observed closely by the audiences over extended periods of time, the critical capacity of soap opera viewers develop into an understanding of the genres, conventions and codes, its narrative structure and appeal and even its cultural marginalisation"[6]. It follows that the very idea of passivity cannot be thrust upon the audience as a general principle even in the case of audiences of mediated drama like soap. Instead, they become active in some way or other and create meanings to the performance.

Fiske goes further and maintains that even audiences of mediated drama cannot be regarded as passive for other reasons. He introduces the concept of "producerly text" in which the production of meaning of television texts is delegated to the viewer. Thus the audience becomes active. In the opinion of Burton, the cultural background of the audience with their particular beliefs, attitude and values also counts much[7]. Needless to say, television serials are also artistic works though diluted in quality for meeting commercial considerations.

Audiences are also divided as spectators, participants and fans. Spectators are in fact, passive audience who "applaud and perhaps involve themselves in the performance ritual, and attendance, but their interaction with the performance's content and performers remains minimal"[8]. On the other hand, participants represent a group likely to be playful or personally committed in one way or other to the entertainment activity. Members of the most die-hard audiences are categorised as fans who enthusiastically support particular music or genre sub-cultures.

Function of Audience in Different Forms of Art: High Culture and Mass Culture

Audience response can be explained on the basis of the division of culture into high culture and mass culture. In the opinion of Gans the term mass culture is a combination of two German terms M*asse* and Kultur. Mass refers to "the non-aristocratic, uneducated portion of European society, especially the people who today might be described as lower middle class, working class and poor". As he adds further, "kultur translates as highculture, it refers not only to the art, music, literature and other symbolic products that were (and are) preferred by the well educated elite of that European society but also to the styles of thought and feelings of those who choose these products—those who are "cultured". Mass culture on the other hand, refers to the symbolic products used by the "uncultured majority".[9] High culture is supposed to be non- commercial, producing a heterogeneous and non-standardised product, and encouraging a creative process by virtue of which it becomes autonomous[10]. Mass culture also possesses cultural autonomy and is not devoid of artistic aura. The size of audience is very small in high culture against large size in mass culture. However, products of high culture are unique in nature with their peculiar structures and codes and formulae. The audience, though educated may not be able to interpret and understand their meaning properly. In turn as Bielby puts, "in high art, an audience member does not make an autonomous personal judgement about the quality of an art form but instead defers to the expert judgement of cultural critics". In other words, the audiences are compelled to surrender their autonomy of interpreting high cultural products. Thus expert or interpreter becomes a key player in high culture. To that extent the standing of the audience of high culture as active gets weakened. On the other hand, the audience of mass culture can understand and appreciate the product without the mediation of an interpreter. In fact, the audiences are more or less familiar with codes and structure of mass cultural products which are invariably standardised like soaps. Any deviation can easily be detected by them. As Bielby adds, "the consumption of mass or popular culture is assumed to be largely unmediated and is based on the consumer's direct experience of the cultural product"[11]. Very often they will be familiar with the narratives, and as he adds further, 'give' for interpreting "the meaning to themselves. In reality, the act of watching for a long period, enables them to understand even the behaviour of different characters"[12].

Mediated dramatic products like films and soaps are standardised products meant to meet the demands of audience. Most of those products fall within the ambit of mass culture, though a few products of high culture can also be found among them. They make use of various techniques to create a favourable impression on the product in the minds of audience as the response of the audience can not be known till it is marketed. One of the usual techniques adopted by them is to hire the services of taste-makers and critics to create a favourable impression in the minds of audience. The experts are supposed to enlighten the audience regarding the quality of the product. However, the critics and taste makers may not always be neutral, or objective. Instead, they may give a biased opinion to favour producers. As Caves adds, "producers and certifiers can cut a mutually profitable secret deal whereby the certifier favours the producer's creative goods in advising the consumer, although not so blatantly that consumer can infer the corruption"[13]. Taking a different stance, Martin Esslin maintains that "what will mean to each member of that collective entity will in turn depend on each individual spectator's 'capacity' or 'competence' to understand or decode the individual signs and sign structure—"[14].

Deviating further in the matter, Hamilton introduces an altogether different concept regarding the characteristics and thereby, the behavioural pattern of audience. In his opinion audience exhibits the characteristics of the members of a crowd. A crowd comprising a multitude of people whose ideas and feelings deviate to a certain single direction and who exhibit a tendency to lose their individual self consciousness in the general self-consciousness of the multitude. He further contends that the crowd has a mind of its own apart from that of any of its individual members[15]. In support of his contention, he borrows the ideas of the French scholar Gustav

Le Ben. As a member of the crowd, the individual is less intellectual, and more emotional than that of his original individual self. To put it in the words of Le Ben, "by the mere fact that he forms a part of the organised crowd, a man descends several rungs in the ladder of civilization"[16]. The behavioural pattern of an individual in the crowd is somewhat similar to that of the proverbial jackal who fell in a pool of coloured water, by which he looked like a wonderful animal, but he could not resist the instinct of howling when other jackals started to howl. Clayton goes on to add that the dramatist who understands the psychology of the crowd which exhibits average intelligence, alone can succeed as a playwright, on which further details were given elsewhere. Needless to say, drama has necessarily to be audience- oriented, if at all it is to be successful.

The Purpose of Viewing or Attending Different Forms of Dramatic performances

Audience participates, or attends a performance to satisfy a need, the unfulfillment of which causes an uneaseiness in their minds. Needs can be utilitarian, or hedonistic, in character. Utilitarian need may relieve stress while hedonistic need leads to enjoyment. Attendance in a drama by and large seems to fulfil hedonistic need.

Now what exactly are the hedonist needs to be satisfied by seeing a drama? Drama is an artistic product. Art is basically the representation of the experience of other people. In the opinion of Fischer, who takes an idealistic stand, each individual wants to be more than his own self. He wants to be a whole man. As Fischer states further, "he feels that he can attain wholeness only if he takes possession of the experience of others that might be potentially his own." By merging with the rest with taking possession of the experience of others, one can attain the fullness of life. Being a representation of the experience of others, art becomes an indispensable means for the merging of the individual with the whole[17].

Instead, when it comes to Bundy, "the value of engaging in a drama experience is that it affords the possibility of aesthetic experience, a particular way of perceiving and knowing the world and our relationship up to it"[18]. To elaborate this, he quotes Jackson who states that "the art offers alternative ways of seeing and understanding the world around us". However, according to Aristotle, the dramatic theoretician of ancient Greece, drama especially tragedy creates a cathartic effect. Naturally, one gets purified by watching a drama. On the other hand, the objective of *abhinya* according to Sanskrit dramaturgy is to "create feeling of bliss or *ananda* in the minds of spectators by revealing various mental states of character. The spectator experiences a feeling of satisfaction and fulfilment"[19]. Apparently, an element of entertainment is inherent in seeing dramatic performances according to Indian approach, against the puritan cathartic stance of Aristotle.

However, according to other authors, the purpose of seeing a drama is much more subtle than the aforesaid stances. In the words of Brandt, "drama is a mirror of life—as a reflection of real human concerns—able to relate individual experiences to an implicit moral structure and scaler of values, able to broaden the viewer's sympathies beyond their moral confines; to lead them to a greater insight into interpersonal and social relationships, to educate their feelings through laughter, suspense, empathy or whatever by means of images as well as words and to do this in a form with a palpable beginning middle and end"[20]. Such theatrical considerations are relevant more to the dramatic performances of high culture than to mass culture. On the other hand, the purpose of visiting mass mediated or popular performances is, by and large, for entertainment. In the words of Martin Esslin "it is regarded as an entertainment, a way to pass time, to be taken out of oneself, to be diverted, distracted"[21]. The vast majority of audiences who watch TV or see a drama during the modern period do so for entertainment. The following passage of Shakespeare aptly describes the situation:

> To wear away this long age of three hours
> Between our after supper and bed time?
> What reveals are in hand? Is there no play
> To ease the anguish of a torturing hour
> —how shall we beguile
> The lazy time if not with some delight.

Brecht also echoes the same when he says that, "it has always been the business of theatre –as all the other arts –to entertain people. This business gives it, its special dignity, it needs no other justification than being fun (spass)- but that justification it must have". He divides entertainment into simple and complex forms. In his opinion, "it is the desire for and expectation of these various forms of simple and complex gratification that bring audience to drama"[22]. Obviously, such a line of thinking corresponds to the attaintment of *ananda* of the Indian approach.

The lazy time of which Shakespeare has spoken of, has widened beyond recognition during recent years. When Shakespeare wrote, only nobles and rich people alone had the luxury of leisure. The ordinary masses were denied of the luxury of leisure time after the day's hard labour. They could rarely attend shows even of rustic nature. On the other hand, they are now endowed with sufficient time for relaxation and leisurely activities. The capacity for paying fees, or other dues, for leisure activities has also improved. The producers of mediated drama have skilfully added various ingredients to increase entertainment elements in their works by using technology which has progressed beyond the imagination of our forefathers. The technologically mediated drama invariably adopts various techniques even in the very format, including the projection of super stars for attracting large number of audience. At the same time, audiences get access to such products very conveniently. Compared to the easy accessibility of mediated drama, theatrical drama can be seen with much difficulty. Naturally, the bulk of audiences would be preferring technologically mediated drama to theatrical drama. Needless to say, theatrical dramas are totally incapable of taking advantage of the new scenario. Nor are they designed to attracta large contingent of audience.

The audiences who thus come to the picture need not necessarily be reckoned as audiences of drama per se. They are a new type of audience created by the mediated drama with the help of advanced technology, by taking advantage of the growing demand for entertainment among the working class. In the terminology of economics, there is a shift in the demand curve to the right. The new class of audience thus created flocks to the cinema halls or sit in front of the TV purely for entertainment. The products they watch are mere commodified forms of some sort of pseudo art, devoid of artistic qualities. Their motivation can be compared to that of the spectators who watch sports and games and who watch the performance for the sake of enjoyment and not for appreciation of the performance. Audiences, who have thus emerged with the new dispensation, cannot be regarded as audience per se of a drama. Instead, it may not be wide the mark, to reckon them as quasi- audience, who squarely embodies the characteristics of a regular consumer and audience proper at the same time. Burton goes one more step and labels them as mere "commodified audience, who are "treated as de-individualised groups of consumers" by nobody other than the industry itself[23].

Changing Role of Audience

As an artistic activity drama encompasses a communication process addressed to an audience. Audience can be active or passive from an artistic point of view. Audience can also be active or passive from an economic angle in the case of drama. Economoc angle assumes importance because drama is a cooperative venture of material and non- material inputs. Producers and thereby inputs have to be supported or sustained by means of material means invariably in the form of money during the modern period. As seen in Chapter 2, artists were sustained by the labour of the slaves and the metics during the ancent Graeco-Roman priod. Drama was sustained by the nobles and the religious bodies when it came to the Middle Ages. They supported drama for their own benefit and not to the benefit of common people. Common people or the masses had to rely on bards and wayside performers to meet their entertainment needs.

Drama acquired a commercial character from the end of the Middle Ages. Financing was done by raising an admission fee from the audience. They thus bcame some sort of active partners in financing dramatic performances also. Financial partnership became stronger when motion pictures arrived in the scene. The situation became a bit more complicated when tele-serials appeared as a new form of drama. As mentioned in Chapter 4, audience does not pay any amount of money for seeing TV programmes. Instead, advertisers foot the bill. Channels charge advertisers on the basis of the size of the audience. As Graeme Burton notes, "the success of the media producer is measured in terms of audience as goods, as much as on the basis of any critical estimation"[24]. The audience who may be capable of finding meanings in the performance, meekly watch the programmes and enable the producer to collect money in his name. What he can do is to switch off the programme, if he is not satisfied. The audience of TV thus becomes passive from an economic angle.

Apparently, the audiences of stage dramas differ very much from that of the audiences of mediated drama. While the audience of stage drama remains as audience proper, what one finds in mediated drama is the transmutation of audience as consumers. Needless to say, what is discernible is the fast growth of the size of the audience of mediated drama against a fall in the case of theatrical drama. An understanding of the characteristics, behavioural pattern and attitude of the audiences in the case of two types of drama can be made by examining their demographic profile, level of education, viewing habits and so on.

Findings of the Field Study

In order to uncover various issues pertaining to audience and to understand their changing profile and behavioural pattern, we have made a survey among audiences. The survey inter-alia covered the socio-economic profile of audiences, their viewing habits and attitude towards drama as well as mediated drama. Altogether 146 number of audiences comprising 86 males and 60 females distributed throughout Kerala were interviewed with structured schedules. Most of them were interviwed in the very venue of the dramatic performances invariably at the time of staging of the drama. The audience selected were those who have seen at least one drama. They have also been viewers of TV and cinema.

The age composition of audience can shed light on the popularity of drama among the different age groups.

Table 7.1: Age Composition of the Audience

Age group	*Males*	*Females*	*Average of the Two*
15-20	1.16	5.0	2.73
21-30	15.72	21.66	18.12
31-40	22.47	28.33	24.83
41-50	33.70	31.66	32.88
51 and above	26.36	13.33	21.47
Total	100	100	100

Normally, it is the youngsters who patronise drama by visiting in large numbers. However, those in the age group 15-20 were the least interested to see stage dramas. Among the males of this group, only 1.16 per cent and of the females only 5 per cent have seen drama during the last one year. With 15.72 per cent of the males and 21.66 per cent of the females seeing a drama, attendance in the age group 21-30 cannot claim to be satisfactory. Those in the age group 31-40, with the males accounting for 22.47 per cent and females accounting for 28.33 per cent cannot claim to be substantial. Those in the age group 41-50 formed the largest group accounting for 33.70 per cent of the males and 31.66 per cent of the females. Among those above 51 years, males formed formed 26.36 per cent and females 13.33 per cent respectively. The middle age group comprising those above 40 years old formed 54.35 per cent of the total. Similar conditions seem to prevail in other parts of the world also. As Harvard journal enjoins, "a youthful generation raised amid digital culture may prove harder to lure to a live theatrical performance; in 2009-10 season, the average Brooadway theatre-goer was 48 years old"[25]. In Kerala they would have developed the habit of seeing drama nearly 20 years back when television was yet to appear or in its formative stage in Kerala. Nevertheless, they seem to retain a keen interest in seeing dramas, in spite of the expansion of television. At the same time, the youngsters who would have patronised dramatic performances seem to be lukewarm towards drama. Among them, the youngest group comprising those below 30 years seems to be the least interested in seeing drama. Instead, they would have been lured by the thrill of mediated drama, especially those offered by the TV.

The educational profile of audience is another factor which indicates the attitude of society at large in respect of the community's preference for different cultural activities.

Table 7.2: Educational Qualification of Different Categories of Audience

Level of Education	*Males*	*Females*	*Total*
Below SSLC	2.32	1.66	2.01
SSLC	25.58	26.66	26.17
Higher Secondary	27.90	18.31	24.87
Degree	24.41	38.33	29.53
P.G	19.76	15.00	17.44
Total	100	100	100

As can be seen from the Table, the majority of the respondents were well educated persons. With 44 per cent of males and 53 per cent of females, degree holders and above accounted for the bulk of the audience. Those whose qualification was below SSLC was only 3.66 per cent among males and 1.66 per cent among females. At the same time, those whose educational qualification was SSLC or Higher Secondary formed 50 per cent. Thus the educational profile was much higher than the state average. Apparently, the educated classes formed the overwhelming majority of the audience. Needless to say, education nurtures a taste and a capacity for appreciation of artistic activities. It is evident that the people who had acquired a taste for drama through education formed the majority of the audience. They would be capable of giving their own interpretation and meaning to the dramas. Apparently, they would fall by and large, within the category of active audience who cannot be labelled as consumers of a mercantile commodity.

Occupational profile forms another criterion which also can shed further light on the characteristics of audience (see Table 7.3).

As can be seen, the respondents were well distributed among various categories of occupations with no particular class dominating the scene. However, Government servants formed one of the largest group with the males among them accounting for about 20.22 per cent of the total. Surprisingly, with 52 per cent, housewives formed the largest numerical group among the females. Though agriculture provides employment for nearly half of the total number people in the state, agricultural classes among the drama going group formed only 14.6 per cent. The ranks of

Table 7.3: Occupational Profile of the Audience

Nature of Occupation	*Males*	*Females*	*Total*
Government servants	20.22	11.47	16.77
Teachers	4.49	4.91	4.69
Pensioners	4.49	—	2.68
Agriculturists	14.60	—	8.72
Business	7.86	3.29	6.04
Engineers	4.49	—	2.68
Mechanics	8.96	—	5.36
Housewives	—	52.45	21.14
Artists	5.61	1.63	4.69
Social activists	1.12	3.91	2.68
Unemployed persons	8.95	—	5.36
Students	5.61	11.47	8.72
Private sector empl	5.61	1.63	3.35
Others	8.00	9.38	7.12
Total	100	100	100

the respondents included pensioners and professionals and students. Artists and social activists formed 4.6 per cent and 2.8 per cent respectively. There were a few unemployed hands among the respondents. Like "the typical Indian theatregoer–conceived as a middle class, educated (though not always professionally trained or employed)", the bulk of the respondents of Kerala also hail from the middle class[26]. The class origin of the audience also resembles to some extent, with that of the theatre audience in Great Britain as revealed in some surveys. In England the middle-class, well educated and financially well to do, formed the bulk of the audience during 1970s[27]].

The number of visits to dramas gives an idea of the respondents' commitment to drama.

Table 7.4: No. of Dramas seen by the Respondents During the Last One Year

No. of Dramas	*Men*	*Women*	*Average of Both*
Nil	4.49	3.33	4.02
1	17.97	10.00	4.76
2	24.71	26.66	25.50
3	15.73	21.66	18.12
4	16.85	10.00	14.09
5	8.98	15.00	8.72
6	4.49	11.66	10.06
7	—	—	—
8	4.49	1.66	3.35
9	—	—	—
10	2.24	—	1.34
Total	100	100	100

The number of visits to theatres gives an indication of the commitment of the audience to drama as an artistic activity. Among the respondents, 4.49 per cent of the males and 3.33 per cent of the females did not see a drama during the last one year though they had an appreciation for drama. Those who were satisfied with seeing one drama consisted of 17.97 per cent of the males and 26.66 per cent of the females. With a combined average of 25.5 per cent, those who saw two dramas formed the largest group among the respondents. Only 15.73 per cent of the males and 21.66 per cent of the females saw three dramas each. Those who saw 4 to 6 dramas during the last one year consisted of 30.32 per cent of the males and 36.66 per cen of the females. Among the respondents 6.73 per cent among the males and 1.66 per cent among the females saw more than six dramas. Apparently, the respondents saw very few number of dramas in an year with more than half of them attending less than three dramas and nobody seeing more than ten dramas. On an average, each person saw 3.17 dramas in a year. Evidently attendance to dramas was very poor even with the so called ardent drama seeing audience. Poor attendance in theatres is a pointer to the declining popularity of drama even with the drama seeing population. Even then, the non- availability of dramatic performances would also be another factor for the poor response to see drama among the respondents.

With the growth of mediated drama those who are interested in drama would also be tempted to see motion pictures. How far they have been enamoured by films was also enquired into. Table 7.5 gives the number of cinemas seen by the respondents.

Table 7.5: Number of Films seen by the Respondents during the Last One Month (%)

No. of films	*Males*	*Females*	*Average of the Two*
Nil	26.96	25.00	26.17
1	3.37	5.00	4.02
2	26.96	13.33	21.47
3	21.34	8.33	16.10
4	15.93	28.33	20.80
5	3.37	15.00	7.54
6 and above	2.24	5.00	3.14

Nearly 74 percent of the respondents saw one film or more during a period of one month with 58.37 per cent seeing 2-4 films. Those who saw five or more films accounted for 10.68 of the total. Only 26.17 per cent did not see at least one film, They would have seen a few films during the course of last one year. Those who saw films would have seen within the range of 12 to 72 films during the course of one year. While the largest number of dramas seen by the respondents did not come upto two digits, the people with least interest in films, saw more than a dozen in an year. At the same time, the average number of films seen by the respondents would have been 2.76 per month. If it were to be so, the average per person for one year would 33.18 films in an year. It follows that the number of films seen by the respondents would be ten times the number of dramas seen.

Time Spent for Watching TV

The time spent for watching TV forms another indicator of the behavioural pattern, of the respondents towards mediated drama.

The respondents who were selected at random from among the audiences of drama have been regularly seeing television also. Those among them who have not seen television during the last month preceding the interview formed only 1.39 percent of the total, and the respondents who saw television for one hour accounted for 28.18 per cent only. Against this, those who watched TV for more than two hours accounted for more than 70 per cent of the total. Moreover, on an average, the respondents spent 1 hour and 53 minutes per day for watching television. It was more than the state average of 1 hour and 48 minutes. Apparently, watching television has become a normal habit even with die-hard adherents of drama. They seem to be more at ease with television than with theatrical drama,

Table 7.6: Time Spent for Watching TV Programmes

Duration of viewing time	*Men*	*Women*	*Average of both*
Not seen	1.12	1.66	1.39
30 minutes	—	1.66	0.33
1 hour	30.33	25.00	28.18
2 hours	55.05	53.33	54.36
3 hours	12.35	10.00	11.40
4 hours	1.12	6.66	3.35
5 and above (hrs)	—	1.66	0.67
Total	100	100	100

The reasons which prompted them to visit theatres contain interesting ideas about the popularity of drama among the respondents. Some of them were attracted by the story, some others were interested to gaze at the process of acting by the artists and a third category of audiences were attracted by the glamour of the artists; the ranking of these three are depicted in Table 7.7.

Table 7.7: Ranking of the Reasons for Attending Dramatic Performance

Reasons for Visiting Theatres	*Men*	*Women*	*Average of the Two*
Interest in the story.	1.12	6.66	3.35
Interest in seeing the process of acting by the artists.	83.31	88.33	83.89
Glamour of artists	—	—	—
Educational message	7.86	3.33	6.04
Others	7.86	1.66	5.40
Total	100	100	100

The audience were asked to list out the reasons for visiting dramatic theatres. All of them were asked to list out different reasons for seeing theatrical dramas. Most of them had different reasons for visiting dramas. Invariably, it seemed that more than one reason would have prompted them to visit drama. The reason which attracted the least number was the interest in the story. It would be due to the poor quality of the literary script. Exceptionally large numbers were interested in the live performance of the artists in person. By evincing keen interest in the very process of acting they seem to identify themselves as partners in drama. The glamour of artists did not form an important reason.

Impact of Television on Audience

An interesting issue relates to the preference of the audience to drama. They were asked to indicate whether they preferred drama in live form or the mediated drama on the television. Table 7.8 indicates the preference of the audience to drama vis-a-vis television

Table 7.8: Audience Preference to Drama *vs.* Television

Drama vs television	*Men*	*Women*	*Average of the Two*
No of respondents who preferred drama	81.05	70	80.5
No of respondents who preferred television	13.15	20	13.5
Those who were indifferent	7.89	10	6.0
Total	100	100	100

Notwithstanding the frequency of visiting or seeing mediated drama, the overwhelming majority of the respondents preferred drama. Only 13.5 per cent favoured television and only 6 per cent was not favouring either of the two. Apparently, the respondents would be rational addicts to theatrical drama. Presumably, it is such a class of die -hard audience who sustain drama as a cultural activity in Kerala. However, TV and other mediated drama have made deep penetration throughout the world. In turn, people all over the world devote a portion of their time for viewing such programmes also. Most of such people would be the new class of audience originated with the overall economic prosperity coupled with the pulling power of the technologically mediated drama.

Some interesting observations were made by the respondents during the field study, regarding their attitude towards stage drama in the context of the popularity of mediated drama. One of them said that the facility for seeing dramas is very limited, though they are interested to see them. Stage performances are done once in a way on special occasions and not frequently. Apparently, they do not have the facility to see drama as and when they want to see it. At the same time, TV is so common and naturally they view them frequently. Furthermore, they can be seen at any time in their own living rooms. On the other hand, they have to go to the theatre located at a distant place to see a drama. In this connection, it is worth recalling what Adoor Gopalkrishnan observed about the shrinking size of dramatic audience. As he put it, "audience have to be invited to see dramas by visiting their homes"[28]. K. Narayana Panicker, whom we met also expressed the need to create and nurture a class of audience for the survival of drma as the general public is lukewarm to see stage drama.

An interesting question asked during the survey was "should drama be encouraged? If so, why?" All the respondents were unanimous in stating that drama should be encouraged and promoted. However, they gave different reasons for promoting drama. One of the respondents regarded drama as a source of employment to a large number of people. Training in drama fosters personality development of children. Problems of life are well reflected in drama. Drama is a training ground for the creation of a better world. The messages which drama conveys are issues of social importance. Drama propagates knowledge through entertainment. Drama represents real lives with their follies and offers guidelines for corrections. Unlike mediated drama, stage drama by itself is a form of art of the ordinary people. Drama nurtures progress in life and creative thinking. Drama provides a training ground for young artists. Drama deserves promotion as it is a multifaceted art form. Another respondent was emphating in stating that drama would survive so long as human life exists. Another respondent expressed that drama would come back.

However, another respondent lamented that timely changes were not introduced in drama.

Conclusion

Notwithstanding such expressions of interest, the size of audience is falling. On the other hand, the size of TV audience is increasing by leaps and bounds. Such a situation cannot be attributed to the abysmal fall in the demand for dramatic performance as such. Instead, it has to be attributed as stated earlier, to the shift in the demand, propelled by various other socio-economic factors like availability of leisue time for the working classes and the increase in the level of income with the ongoing economic development. With the availability of leisure time, the demand for meeting the entertainment need has become very strong. The dramatic theatres which served the entertainment need, seem to be totally inadequate to meet this growing demand. There was some sort of a vacuum in the field of entertainment. The timely arrival of mediated drama like films and TV has filled this gap. The size of the audience which has grown with such developments is being skillfully lured by TV and films. A number of other reasons can also be attributed to this "colonisation of leisure time" by TV. As mentioned earlier, the basic reason for seeing dramas even in the past was that it offered a means to pass the time. Artistic quality could enthuse only a minority of audience. If at all, a large number of people attended drama in the past, the motive with most of them seems to have been the absence of other forms of entertainment. Entry of mediated drama has effectively solved this problem. At the same time, the themes and genres of TV and film can be suitably modified with an eye on capturing the attention of the audiences. Drama per se, cannot be modified in such a way as to attract the attention of theviewrs.

Unlike other forms of art, drama calls for fairly good amount of money cost for for securing the services of different forms of input. How the cost is to be recouped and by whom are issues of paramount importance in the presentation of stage drama. In the past, drama was supported by the nobles or public authorities. They supported it for their own purpose and the means required for the performances came from the toils of slaves or yeomen. With the commercialisation of art which ensued from 16 th century, the patronage of drama was thrust upon the audience by charging an admission fee. There was a feeling that audience would behave like the consumer in the market disregarding the distinctive characteristics of the audience. Nevertheless, the system worked for some time. However, once mediated drama appeared in the scene, the support from the audience dwindled with the consumer- audience abandoning drama leaving drama to the actual audience. However, the number of dramatic audience per se, is totally insufficient to render sufficient material support to drama.

The issue before any audience is, as to why he should travel all the way to the theatre located at a long distance for seeing the drama for which he has to pay ticket charge also. Even those who were devoted to drama opted to see serials because TV has emered as part of life with facilities to see it very conveniently. Ultimately, the lure of the mediated drama like the cinema or television outweighs regular drama in the commercial sense in spite of its artistic quality. In sum, it is the economic factors which tilt the scale in favour of mediated drama.

However, the artistic element remains intact. There are some who are still enamoured with the artistic side of drama. They are not able to meet the cost arising on account of the application of different inputs. Market which guides economic activities fails to meet the need for financing drama. How to surmount such a piquant situation is uncovered in the next Chapter.

NOTES AND REFERENCES

1. Fischer Ernst (1957); *The Necessity of Art: A Marxist Approach* (Translated by Anna Bostock, Penguin Books) p. 210.
2. Hancock, Alan (1968); *Mass Communication* (London, Longman Green & Co.) p. 67.
3. Dharwadker Apara Bhargava (2005); quotes from Tendulkar; See Dharwadker Aparna Bhagava (2005); *Theatres of Independence* (New Delhi, Oxfrd University Press) p. 113.
4. Wolfgang Iser (2010); "Interaction between Text and Reader" in Colins Jane; *Theatre and Performance Design: A Reader in Scenography;* (New York, Routledge) p. 423.
5. Abercrombie, Nicholas (*1996*); *Television and Society* (Cambridge, Polity Press) p. 7.
6. Denise, D. and William. P. Bielby (2004); "AudienceAesthetics and Popular Culture" in Friedland and MohrJohn (Eds.); *Matters of Culture: Cultural Socilogism Practice* (Cambridge, University Press) see pp. 303-305.
7. Graeme Burton (2010); *Media and Society; Cultural Perspectives* (New York, Tata McGraw & Hill), p. 87.
8. Sayre Sahay (2008); *Entertainment Markrting and Communication* (New Delhi, Pearson Education Inc.), p. 106.
9. Gans Herbert J. (1974); *Popular Culture and High Culture: An Analysis and Evaluation of Taste* (New York, Basic Books) p. 10.

10. Gans Herbert J. (1974); *op. cit.*, p. 21.
11. Denise D. and Y. William. P. Bielby (2004); "*Audience Aesthetcs and Popular Culture" in Friedland* Roger and Mohr John (2004) *Matters of Culture; Cultural Sociology in Perspective* (Cambridge, University Press) p. 308.
12. Denise D. and William. P. Bielby (2004); *op. cit.*, p. 303.
13. Caves Richard (200); *Creative Industries: Contract between Art and Commerce* (Harvard University Press) p. 1190.
14. Esslin, Martin (1987); *The Field of Drama* (*New York, Metheun*) p. 128.
15. Hamilton Clayton (2004); *The Theory of the Theatre, and Other Principles of Dramatic Criticsm* (Project Gutenburg Online Book Catalogs) p. 12.
16. M. Gustave Le Bon (1996); *The Crowd: A Study of the Popular Mind* (Project Gutenberg E-Text of the Crowd) p. 15.
17. Fischer Ernst (1984); *Necessity of Art: A Marxist Approach* Translated by Anna Bostock (Penguin Books) pp. 7-9.
18. Bundy Penny; "Aesthetic Engagement in Drama Process" in *Research in Drama Education*, Vol. 8 No. 2.
19. Jain Nemichandra (1992); *Indian Theatre: Tradition, Continuity and Change* (New Delhi, Vikas Publishing Company) p. 25.
20. Thorham Sue and Purvit Tony (2005); *Television Dramas, Theories and Identities* (Palgrave Mcmillan, inc) 22.
21. Esslin Martin (1987); *op. cit.*, p. 130.
22. Esslin, Martin (1987); *op. cit.*, p. 132.
23. Burton Graeme (2010); *Media and Society: Cultural Perspective* (New York, Tata McGraw Hill) p. 98.
24. Burton Graeme (2010); *op. cit.*, p. 87.
25. Harvard Magazine (2012); *The Future of Theater in a Digital Age, Ranging from Non to Broadways*, p. 2.
26. Dharwadker, Aparna Bhargava (2005); *Theatre of Independence: Drama Theory and Urban Performance in India Since 1947* (Oxford University Press) p. 105.
27. Allen John (1979): "The Effects of Subsidy on Western European Theatre in the 1970s" in James Redmond (ed.); *Drama and Society* (Cambrdge, University Press) p. 108.
28. *Malayala Manorama*; (Newspaper, Kottayam) dated 21-09-2014.

8

Policy Options for the Survival of Dramatic Theatres

Dramatic theatres face stiff competition from the technologically mediated drama. The difficulties stem from different angles. As seen in Chapter 5, they are not able to recoup the cost of production in many instances which were examined during the field study. At the same time, talented artists seek their fortune in the newly evolved technologically-mediated drama like films and tele-serials. Of late, the majority of the audiences who used to patronise dramas for long, have also deserted drama. Even then, dramatic theatres manage to survive, though with depleted sustaining power. In such a situation, how theatrical drama manages to survive comes to the fore as a major problem calling for serious investigation.

Drama is one of the oldest forms of art created by man. Almost all societies had some sort of dramatic performance from the ancient past. Theatrical drama in its present form is the outcome of its evolution over the years. What is attempted in a drama is the representation of the life of man by narrating a real or imaginary story to an audience in such way as to catch their attention. The meaning of life can be understood and even appreciated in a better way by seeing drama. It also entertains people. With the ongoing economic development, the demand for entertainment is on the increase. Theatrical drama has its own limitations for meeting the growing demand for entertainment, stemming from the easy availability of leisure time even with the ordinary people. Actually, each dramatic performance is a separate product which can be repeated only as a new performance, even if the same actors appear in the stage on another occasion. Apparently, drama cannot be enacted as and when it is needed, even with extra cost and effort.

However, the epoch making achievements in technology has paved the way for the production of drama on factory lines. Such technologically mediated drama as they are called, can present the dramatic scenes in an exemplary manner by applying various technological devices, The entrepreneurs who produce mediated drama could take advantage of the growing demand for entertainment by reproducing feature films and tele-serials at very low marginal cost with the aid of technology and exhibiting them at very low price. Thus technologically mediated drama could steal a march over theatrical drama. If it were to be so, the questions posed are: (i) What exactly is the gravity of the threat from mediated drama?; (ii) Can theatrical drama survive the challenge from the mediated drama?; (iii) An equally important question is, should drama be protected from the onslaught of the technologically mediated drama?; and (iv) If so, what should be the policy options for protecting theatrical drama?

The threat from the mediated drama stems basically from the economies of scale in production. The products of mediated drama can be supplied to a large number of people in a very convenient manner. In the case of a feature film, any number of prints or cubes can be produced at will with very low cost from an original play. It can be exhibited simultaneously in a number of places for any number of days at zero variable cost of production. A typical Malayalam film is being normally released with not less than 50 cubes. They can, therefore be exhibited simultaneously in 50 theatres. Other language films like Hindi or Tamil are released in 1000 stations or more on the very first day. It is reported, for instance, that a film produced in December 2014 by Rajani Kanth, a Tamil matinee hero was released simultaneously in 2500 stations. Assuming that a popular Malayalam film is seen at least by 300 people on the very first day in one station, at least 15000 people would have seen it on the very first day of release. There are at present well over 600 theatres in Kerala. In such conditions, the film would be seen by not less than 180000 people, if it is exhibited for one day in all theatres. Films will be exhibited for a number of days depending on the popularity. Assuming that it will run on an average for three days, the film would have been seen by at least 540000 audiences. Thus on an average, film would have been seen by not less than 500000 audiences[1]. If, it is sufficiently popular the exhibition will continue with more and more audiences seeing it. Against such massive turn over of audiences for feature films, what exactly would be the size of audience for a theatrical drama? On no account, it can attract more than 500 audiences for the first performance, provided it is sufficiently popular. If it is to be presented again, the actors would have to stage it afresh in the same theatre by incurring extra cost and effort. In order to be seen by an audience numbering 100000 it will have to be staged afresh at least for two hundred days or more. It is reported that the audience strength does not normally exceed, 15000 even with repeated staging. Apparently, a film can attract audiences numbering 30 times or more the size of audiences of a drama. As Mcgrath, a leading producer and distributor enjoins, "you can open a movie on 1000 screens or, 5000 screens, but a Broadway show is limited by the capacity of the theatre"[2]. Since such hurdles have to be faced apart from the apathy of the audience and the actors, it will be well neigh impossible for drama to compete with films. In the case of tele-serials a Malayalam episode of half an hour would have been seen at least by one lakh audiences on the very first day.

Technologically mediated drama is on a stronger wicket for other reasons as well. By applying advanced technology they can create make-believe situation appropriate to each scene in a better way. Furthermore, as Encyclopaedia Britannica enjoins, "in films and television, mistakes can be eliminated, unsuccessful scenes can be reshot and rewritten and the whole work can be manipulated, edited, and set before the public with every detail in place"[3]. Management and marketing can be undertaken with better business strategy and success. Furthermore, as seen in Chapter 6, mediated drama is able to lure talented actors and other artists to their fold by offering fabulous sums as remuneration. Money minded artists look upon the career in television and film as better options. Most audiences on their part, flock to the show on account of the aura of the actors. Majority of the films are invariably studded with superstars possessing mesmeric hold over the audience. On the other hand, theatrical drama has to contend with less talented actors invariably of mediocre calibre. Audiences would naturally prefer the performances of gifted actors and super stars to the performance of actors of theatrical drama.

With the growing affluence, consumerism has gained unprecedented ascendancy in all parts of the world. Entertainment activities have also grown in a big way in tandem with consumerism. The ordinary people on their part, evince interest to see a show purely for entertainment. They are least bothered about the artistic qualities or originality of the play. In fact, what the mediated drama offers to the audience is nothing but a standardised commodity suitable for meeting the entertainment needs. They conveniently display sceneries with appropriate spectacles capable of attracting attention of audiences. Thus mediated dramas of standardised variety with stronger pulling power easily lure the bulk of the audiences.

Side by side, they spend huge amounts of money for advertisement. Through advertisement, they manage to widen the demand of the audience. Even people who are not interested in drama are lured to see technologically mediated drama through effective advertisement. Dramatic theatres do not possess enough financial strength to spend on advertisements. The competition between the two thus becomes uneven and dramatic theatres do not have the wherewithal to face the onslaught of mediated drama.

Apart from such poor sustaining power, dramatic theatres are susceptible to another difficulty. In the context of competition with mediated drama, dramatic theatres land themselves in a situation under which their products fall in quality let alone in attraction. As mentioned earlier, the theatres have to be content with the services of less gifted artists, as most of the skilled artists seek their fortune with the mediated drama. Furthermore, most of the theatres are of amateur category. The prevalence of such theatres with less gifted artists in their rolls, as Hilda Baumol maintains, "restricts the opportunities to experiment, limiting the character of plays, and the content of musical programmes—. It involves cutting of corners in terms of quality of performers when their high salaries threaten budgets, in terms of rehearsal time, and in terms of freedom of artistic choice"[4]. In other words, manifestation of what has been called artistic deficit becomes apparent.

Reasons for Promoting Dramatic Theatres

Notwithstanding the growing popularity of the technologically mediated drama, theatrical performances, as already indicated, do have a niche in the world of art and culture. In various parts of our own country, theatres are alive and kicking. The presence of large number of dramatic clubs and banners stands as a clear manifestation of the prevalence of theatres in Kerala state. If so, why they are active and virulent, in spite of the powerful challenge from the technologically mediated drama?

In the words of Oscar Wilde, "drama forms the greatest of all art forms, the most immediate way in which a human being can share with another the sense of what it is to be a human being"[5]. Though it has faced upheavals on various occasions in the past, it has successfully weathered such storms and succeeded to remain as time tested cultural form. Dramatic performances are representations of human life enshrined with aesthetic value. Audiences, in whose front the performances are staged, enrich themselves by experiencing aesthetic value when they see a drama in live form. Representation of human life attempted in the technologically mediated drama is a mere reproduction of the original. It can, in no way be a match to theatrical drama as embodiments of aesthetic value and cultural quality. As Kuspit maintains, aesthetic experience is precluded by the second hand experience of art in reproduction, whether it is electronically advanced or mechanically outmoded reproduction of mediated drama[6]. Furthermore, as mentioned earlier, they are mere mercantile commodities turned out for satisfying the entertainment needs on factory lines by the so called culture industry. Horkheimer Max and Adorno, who coined the term culture industry, were annoyed at the manner in which arts like drama are produced on commercial lines with the aid of advanced technology. They simply condemned such products of culture industry as "corrupt" form of art "dedicated to elevated pleasure". In so doing, they add further, "art renounces its own autonomy and proudly takes its place among consumption goods"[7]. Such consumption goods are produced as standardised products on a massive scale with least regard to the uniqueness expected of artistic creation. Though it need not always be so pessimistic, as Horkheimer and Adorno portrayed, "the styles and devices of film" to put it in the words of Dharwadker, "can never supplant the literary and communal properties of drama proper"[8]. Furthermore, mediated drama, as seen in Chapter 7, has ttransformed the audience as mere consumers of a mercantile commodity. On the other hand, audience in a drama remains basically as partners capable of appreciating its artistic qualities and in so doing, they may serve incidentally as a source for meeting part of the cost for staging a drama. (Nevertheless, the fall in the box office collection associated with the onslaught is being looked upon as a question mark on the survival of drama). Thus, the rivalry between the two amounts to some sort of a competition between an artistic product and a mercantile product. Needless to say, the superior standing of theatrical drama as a artistic product to which the audiences of active mould pay heed ensures its survival from the challenge of mediated drama. Furthermore, as seen in Chapter 6, some of the devoted artists also lend a helping hand to the survival of drama. In short the relation between the two as Dharwadker maintains "will be one of competition and mutual exclusion rather than significant interchange"[9].

Variety is, after all the spice of life. Art world can be compared to a beautiful garden with a wide variety of plants. The presence of shrubs, creepers, flowering plants and a few giant trees, etc., make it attractive and beautiful. Mediated drama which stands like a tall tree offers only standardised products meant to meet the entertainment needs of the ordinary consumer. There can be demand for variety, which a limited number of films, or tele-serials, may not be able to meet. In Malayalam, for example, only 140 films were produced in 2014. The audiences have no choice, but to be content with those 140 films which function like the Procustrean bed. Theatrical drama on the other hand can offer variety and satisfy the tastes of varying category of audiences. As Encyclopaedia Britannica enjoins, "dozens of immortally great expressions of human spirit have been written for performance by live actors for live audience and cannot be adequately experienced in any other medium. This is why despite economic challenges, limited technical resources and funding and the logistical problems of touring, the live theatres must survive"[10].

Skills and talents are not uniformly distributed within a given population. Only the best actors are promoted by the technologically mediated drama as they look upon shows as pure business enterprises. They can provide opportunity for a limited number of artists. The 140 films produced in Malayalam in 2014, could provide opportunity for, at the most, 1500 artists. Only the best could find a place in those films. In the words of Baumol, mediated drama has "limited the market for performers by permitting a few groups to reach audiences which formerly could be served by a large number of performers"[11]. The large number of aspiring artists would find themselves with no opportunuity to express their creative talents. Dramatic theatres can provide opportunities to more number of actors, some of them with less talents, to give expression of their artistic inspirations. Similarly, local needs and local talents get an opportunity to fulfil their desires through theatrical dramas. Festivals and carnivals are a regular phenomenon in our country. Dramatic performances add lustre to these ceremonies. It also provides a training ground to young artists. Some of them after starting their innings in dramatic theatres, can hope to get opportunities in the mediated drama,

Dramatic theatres receive fairly good amount of support from public authorities apparently for tiding over their poor bargaining power in the market. Such doles from the state forms another contributory factor for their survival. If so, what would be the grounds for the payment of doles is the question.

The Policy Options

As already mentioned, the main problem of dramatic theatres stems from the difficulty in raising enough finance to meet the cost. The support from audience who used to subscribe dramatic performances weakened with the emergence of mediated drama. In turn, public support is sought as the only way out to tide over the difficulties.

Public support to performing arts including dramatic performances has been a live issue even before the entry of technologically mediated drama. The issue has attracted scholarly attention culminating in the formulation of the well-known concept, "cost disease of performing arts". It was put forward by Baumol and William Bowen in their book *Performing Art: The Economic Dilemma,* published in 1966. Baumol and Bowen maintain that the cost of production of arts remains stable while it falls in the case of manufacturing industry with technological progress. While other sectors are the beneficiaries of technological progress with which cost of production can be reduced by applying various labour saving methods, art, by its very nature, is not in a position to effect labour saving methods and thereby to raise productivity. In turn, cost of production of works of art remains stable, or assume, a rising trend in the case of labour charges at a time when the cost in other sectors falls. As the authors state, "the faster general pace of technological advance, the greater will be the increase in overall wage level and the greater the upward pressure on cost in those industries which do not enjoy increased productivity"[12]. Such an anomalous pattern calls for public support for art. Though they have clubbed actors and other artists as mere labourers in contravention to the exalted position as creative workers they have suggested the need for public support to performing arts. As Baumol and Bowen conclude, "increased support from other sources will have to be found if the performing arts are to continue their present role in the cultural life—"[13]. With the advent of mediated drama in a big way, the need for subsidy to performing arts has emerged as a major issue calling for serious attention for supporting theatres.

Some authors have, however, expressed apprehension regarding the rationale for subsidising theatres. One line of argument is that only a minority of the population is benefitted by the payment of subsidy, as very few people care to see theatrical performance. Even Baumol and Bowen concede that, "the most basic objection to government support to performing art is simply that those who want to see them ought to pay the price. —one commentator went on to say 'If opera cannot pay for itself, the fault is with opera'—it has never been a principle of our society that the people as a whole should be forced to pay for the entertainment of a few—"[14]. In some cases, undeserving performances also stomach a major portion of the subsidy. Another line of thinking is that subsidy is granted without taking into consideration the opportunity cost of staging a drama.

It follows that the benefit which society gains should be higher than the cost to the society by subsiding theatres. Empirical evidences have to be sought on this matter which may prove to be a difficult proposition. Nevertheless, some studies made in Great Britain, indicate that "RSC gives a benefit of cost ratio of 1.18 i.e. every pound of subsidy returns 1.18 in benefit"[15]. Yet, another ground for opposing subsidy stems from the doubt regarding its effectiveness in promoting genuine works of art. The exponents of such a line of thinking go to the extent of maintaining that subsidy can be harmful for the growth of genuine works of art. As an author puts, "one might argue that—the subsidised theatre is a main culprit in continually revisiting traditional works at the expense of the new"[16]. Furthermore, as the government cannot distinguish between good and bad art, even bogus firms or pseudo-artists may take advantage of the situation by amassing subsidy. State may try not to promote such works which are not beneficial to the society by imposing certain conditions.

Under such circumstances, the conclusion of one study is as follows: "yet even though not necessarily socially optimal, some subsidy can be shown to be economically justified, but only in the narrow institutional context of the status quo". It goes on to maintain that "in short the case for continued arts subsidy is not certainly compelling, especially with regard to the alleged external consumption benefits, and the absence of real evidence presented for the persistence of Baumols'cost disease"[17]. Even Baumol feels that most of the grounds on which public support for the performing arts can be justified seem to be weak[18]. Similarly, after examining various pros and cons of subsidy, another author concludes that justifications, "have been found lacking when considered analytically or empirically in the rigorous free market frame work of economists"[19].

Though empirical evidences of free market economists are scanty, there are enough grounds for subsidising theatrical drama for the reasons indicated earlier. In fact, market rationalty, as reflected through the price level, does not correspond to the society's preference. The actual market prices are determined by the preferences of the rich consumers, while the consumers with very little income do not have any chance to indicate their choice. As Baumol and Bowen add "government funds intended to promote equality of opportunity directly or indirectly may be vied as a means for improving the way in which the market election is conducted"[20]. Survival of the fittest may sound well according to the pure market oriented economic rationality. However, considerations of ethics and humanitarian values also count much in public policy options. Moreover, arts are public goods which render benefits in excess of the receipts one can hope to collect at the box office. At the same time, dramatic performances create not merely economic value but also cultural value. Needless to say, cultural value does not behave in tandem to economic considerations alone. On the other hand, rational addiction becomes more relevant in such cases. Under such circumstances, it "becomes a response to one of the needs of the society at large" to promote dramatic theatres[21]. As Bowen enjoins "the arts are public goods whose benefits demonstrably exceed the receipts one hope to collect at the box office"[22]. They also form a constituent unit of what is known as merit goods. According to a study made by Throsby and Withers in Australia, merit good considerations have been the most significant single explanation of government involvement in the arts[23]. Similarly, public support will contribute to the preservation of national heritage.

Mode of Public Support to Drama

The mode of support to drama differs from country to country. The US which stands as the citadel of technologically mediated drama has been following a laissez- faire policy for a long period in so far as public support to drama is concerned. A policy change favouring aid to art was adopted only during 1960s. Even then, the volume of state aid remains rather meagre. The main source of aid continues to be private philanthropists and corporate bodies. Nevertheless, federal government gives some tax concessions to those institutions which render any aid to art. An American author T. Moore states emphatically "that the best method of furnishing such aid for the sake of a free, unfettered theatre would be tax exemption"[24]. Local bodies also support art by giving certain facilities like building grant to theatre and so on.

West European countries on the other hand maintain a liberal tradition of giving aid to theatre. The quantum of aid varies from country to country. Germany tops the list among the countries which subsidise theatre. Subsidy forms the means by which the British theatre industry became the strongest in the whole world in terms of export earnings as a chief tourist attraction. At present, the funds derived from a national lottery are being substituted for direct government support[25]. France also provides aid to theatre on a liberal scale, though the state has imposed rigid supervision of the national art institutes.

India is one of the countries which subsidises dramatc theatres on a fairly liberal scale with the intention of promoting them. Since independence, the government of India as well as the state governments have started institutions like the School of Drama, Sangeeta Nataka Academy, Lalitha Kala Academy, etc. One method is to grant subsidy on a limited scale to the theatres for covering a major portion of the cost. Cost of construction of theatres and dramatic festivals are supported by the state. Public also are encouraged to promote dramatic theatres. The Ministry of Culture at the Centre and the Department of Culture at the state level function as nodal agencies in granting aid to theatres.

One option which can be adopted in India is to provide subsidy on a local basis. Since dramas meet local demand and promote local talents, local bodies can be designated as the nodal agencies for distributing help to the theatres. Subsidy to drama can very well be included as part of the development plans of local bodies. Such a pattern seems to prevail in Germany with considerable degree of success.

Another method is to organise dramatic festivals during certain periods of the year. They are being organised successfully in many parts of the world. Films which may not require so much support are also being promoted throughout the world by organising film festivals. Side by side, dramatic clubs or organisations are being formed for promoting and safeguarding dramatic theatres. They operate as non- profit dramatic organisations.

Dramatic theatres can survive with the revival of classic dramas. Theatrical clubs and festivals can be the agencies which can sustain them with considerable degree of success. Shakespearean dramatic theatre is a classical example which renders yeomen service in this regard. Similarly, dramatic festivals made in honour of veteran dramatists as is done in honour of Jagathy N.K. Achary Memorial Dramatic Festival etc., in Kerala can be another method for safeguarding and promoting drama

The most important step would be to promote new types of dramatic genres. As already indicated, drama in the present form was evolved after changes and modifications were adopted at different periods. The present form is not the final stage and it can be modified. Different forms are being adopted in various countries. Models of Asian or African types can be adopted with suitable changes. Similarly, some of the old forms of performances are getting popularity with the blurring of the distinction among the social classes. In many parts of the world, there is also a revival of interest in folk arts. As a matter of fact, "elite interest in folk forms generated new audiences for such forms and helped save traditions around the world that might otherwise have succumbed to industrialisation and cultural globalisation"[26]. It may not be out of place, to point out that the the attempts of persons like Bidal Sirkar or K.N. Panicker to promote traditional types of performances do have a positive impact in sustaining dramatic theatres. Dharwadker endorces the same, with the statement that Sircar's "third theatre offers the most fully developed Indian conception of dramatic medium as a live, induplicable mode of human communication that creates fictions that are not constrained by verisimilitude"[27].

In sum, the fusion of spiritual and material means in the creation of artistic activities like drama justifies the payment of subsidy to them. Though economic rationality stands in the way of granting subsidies, artistic considerations calls for the payment of subsidy to such products. After all, drama is an artistic activity by all standards, though material means are needed to perform them. Provision for the survival of drama in the future calls for support in the present. Interestingly, motion pictures and tele-serials are the recepients of state support though they are basically commercial products relying on advanced technology. Ipso facto, dramatic theatres have a better claim to get financial support from the state.

NOTES AND REFERENCES

1. Information gathered from Dr. C.S. Venkiteswaran, Film Critic.
2. http://harvardmagazine.com/2012/01//the-future-of-theater; p. 4.
3. Encyclopaedia *Britannica* Theatre (art); *Search for Audience.*
4. *Baumol and* Bowen: "On the Peforming Arts; the Anatomy of their Economic Problems" in Towse Ruth (ed.) (1997); *Baumols Cost Disease* (Cheltenham, Edward Elgar) p. 50.
5. quoted by Vikas Shah in "Theatre, Performance and Society/Thought Economics" in http:// thougteconomcs.blogspot.in /2014/03/thetre-performance-society.html
6. Kuspit Donald; "Per Contra: Paradoxes and Problems of Reproduction and Commodification of Art in the Age of Capitalist Reproduction" http: www.per contra.net/archive/19kuspit.in
7. Adorno, T.W. and Horkheimer Max (1977); "The Culture Industry: Enlightenment as Mass Deception" in Curran James (ed.): *Maas Communication and Society* (London, Open University) see pp. 365-76.
8. Dharwadker Aparna Bhargava (2008); *Theatres of Independence* (Delhi, Oxford Unversity Press) p. 124.
9. Dharwadker Aparna Bhargava (2008); *op. cit.*, p. 125.
10. Encyclopedia Britainnica; *Theatre (art) Search for Audience.*
11. Baumol. W.J. (1976); "Preface: Recent Developments in the Economics of the Performing Arts" in Blaug Mark, *The Economics of the Art* (London, Martin Roberson & Company) p. 4.

12. W.J. Baumol and W.G. Bowen (1997); "On the Performing Arts: The Anatomy of Their Economic Problems" Reprinted in Ruth Towse; *op. cit.*, p. 48.
13. W.J. Baumol and W.G. Bowen (1966); reproduced in Ruth towse *op. cit.*, p. 50.
14. Baumol W.J. and W.G. Bowen (1966); "Arguments for Public Support of the Performing Arts" in Balaug Mark (ed.); *The Economics of the Arts* (London, Martin Robertson) p. 47.
15. Collins Alan and Hand Chris (1998); "Making a Crisis out of a Drama: Should we Continu Public Financial Supportfor the British Theater?" in *Economic Issues* Vol. 3, Part 2 Sept. 1998 p. 26.
16. Collins Alan and Hand Chris (1998); *op. cit.,* p. 25.
17. Collins Alan and Hand Chris (1998); *op. cit.,* p. 26.
18. Baumol William J. "Performing Arts" in Ruth Towse (ed.); *Baumol's Cost Disease: The Arts and Other Victims* (Cheltenham, Eward Elgar) p. 100.
19. Fullerton Don (1991); "On Justification for Public Support of Arts" in *Journal of Cultural Economics*, Vol. 15, No. 2, Dec. 1991.
20. W.J. Baumol and W.G. Bowen (1966); "Arguments for Public Support to Performing Arts" Blaug Mark (1976); *op. cit.*, p. 50.
21. W.J. Baumol and W.G. Bowen (1966) in Mark Blaug (ed.); *op. cit.*, p. 55.
22. Bowen Williams (1966); "On the Rationale of Public Support" in *Performing Arts: The Economic Dilemma* (The Twentieth Century Fund Reproduced in Towse Ruth (ed). *Baumol's Cost Disease* (Cheltenham, (London, Edward Elgar) p. 260.
23. Quoted from Throsby and Withers by Heilburn and Gray Charles. M. (2001); *The Economics of Art and Culture* (Cambridge University Press) p. 242.
24. T. Moore (1976); *"Reasons for Subsidizing American Theater"* in Blaug Mark; *The Economics of Art* (London, Martin Robertson London) p. 40.
25. *Encylopaedia Britannica* (2014); *The Role of Subsidy.*
26. *Encyclopaedia Britannica* (2014); *The Place of Theatre in the Contemporary Life.*
27. Dharwadker Aparna Bargava (2008); *The Theatres of Independence* (Oxford University Press) p. 123.

9

Summary and Conclusions

Drama is one of the oldest forms of art which entertains, educates and enlivens people all the world. Almost all classes of people had some sort of dramatic performance. Unlike the other forms of art, drama is a joint product of a host of artists and non-artists. The playwright, the actor, the musician, the dancer, the director and the make-up man contribute their talents in some form or other to stage a drama. Furthermore, material means like the make up materials, the stage with the theatre and even ordinary labour input come to the fore for each performance. In other words, it is a Janus- faced cultural service in which artistic skill and material means come to the picture in the staging of a drama. In turn, cost element becomes a major determinant in any drama. How to meet the cost has been a major issue from the very beginning. Apparently, economic dimension became an integral part of a drama.

Technology has been a hand maid to all human endeavours from the dawn of civilisation. Light and sound entered as essential ingredients to drama once the technological know-how to tame them was mastered. With the inventions of photography and the discovry of the principle of persistent vision, far reaching changes were on the anvil in many forms of art including drama. It did not take much time first, for the invention of motion pictures and then tele-serials. They are nothing but photographs of dramatic performances which can be exhibited or relayed at will in various places at different occasions. Such pictures are not merely natural in appearance, but also very attractive as they are produced with the aid of advanced technology. They are produced on factory-lines encompassing economies of scale and accordingly they fall within the ambit of the so called culture industry of the scholars of Frankfurt school. In fact, some authors go on to maintain that such technologically mediated drama forms a new kind of art-the seventh art.

Since they can be reproduced at very little marginal cost, they can be exhibited at very low price to the audience. At the same time, they can be exhibited at multiple points. Audience can therefore watch or gaze them very conveniently and in the case of tele-serials by sitting in their own drawing rooms. In turn, they offer stiff competition to dramatic theatres with the result that there has been a serious erosion in the size of audience of the stage drama. The question then is, can drama survive the challenge from the technologically mediated drama? Notwithstanding the challenge from the mediated drama, dramatic theatres seem to survive in almost all parts of the world. If so, the question is, what is the raison d'etre for the survival of dramatic theatres? The present study is therefore an attempt to uncover the deeper implications of the challenge to dramatic theatres from the technologically mediated drama and to enquire into the factors at work which sustain drama as an art.

As a starting point, the problems were identified, the conceptual frameworks drawn up and the research issues earmarked in the Introduction. A plethora of concepts like base-superstructure dichotomy, culture industry, Janus -faced cultural service, cultural discount etc., come to the fore as suitable formulations for uncovering various facets relating to the study. It was postulated that dramatic theatres survive on account of the insistent urge on the part of the creative artists to maintain their freedom of expression on the one hand and on the other, to the material and moral support of the active audience, despite the strong pulling power of the technologically mediated drama. The study was designed to proceed with an interdisciplinary approach by drawing elements from sister disciplines like art, culture, economics, and sociology with main emphasis on economics of culture. It was proposed to examine the issues by taking empirical evidences from the experience of Malayalam drama.

The study proceeds with a brief overview of the evolution of drama over the years in Chapter 2. Drama, as a cultural form, had its origin in ancient Greece, where it has emerged as an offshoot of the festival of Dionysus, the god of fertility. The festival used to commence with a procession to the temple in honour of the god followed by dithyramb by bands of chorus. Subsequently, dramatic performance in the form of tragedy was introduced. Eminent dramatists like Euripides, Sophocles, Aeschylus wrote and staged a number of tragedies during 5th century BC at the time of the festival. Comedies and farces were also staged in course of time. The performances were attended by the whole body of citizens and the people of Hellenic origin from other parts of Greece. When it came to the time of Roman hegemony, not much importance was assigned to dramas per se, though some reputed authors were credited with having written a good number of dramatic works. Romans preferred sports, amusements, boxing, gymnastics, rope dancing etc. Nevertheless, they constructed some theatres like Colosseum for staging the performances. By and large, rich citizens aided with the muscular strength of the slaves under their command provided the much needed material inputs for dramatic performance during the Graeco-Roman period. Dramatic performances per se, did not get sufficient importance during the Medieval period and there was actually a serious decline in dramatic activities. Nevertheless, religious dramas were staged in the vicinity of churches, very often by the priests. Ordinary people could meet their entertainment needs from the bards and other troupes travelling in different parts of Europe.

Theatrical drama received a boost with the Renaissance in Europe. In almost all parts of Europe, dramatic performances on the lines of Greek drama began to reappear. One notable development was the emergence of commercial consideration as an important motive behind dramatic performances. Kings and nobles were in the field to promote drama not for its artistic importance but for enhancing their own name and fame. Dramatic troupes also used to travel in different parts of Europe. Dramatic activities spread in the US by 18th century. Performance was invariably staged by the European actors, rather than by the indigenous Americans. Emergence of star system was another development of the period. Dramtic theatres, were looked upon as commercial ventures, with a leading actor occupying the helm of affairs.

The entry of technologically mediated drama of culture industry forms the theme of Chapter 3. With the spectacular development in technology, the possibility for producing works of art on factory lines became a reality. The process by which culture is produced on factory lines is termed culture industry. Motion pictures and tele-serials form the main components of the technologically mediated drama of culture industry. They are mere pictures of dramatic performances exhibited to the audience. However, they are able to offer stiff competition to dramatic theatres on account of the application of superior technology in every stage of production and of the suitability for exhibiting at multiple points with practically very little marginal cost.

Dramatic tradition of India and the pattern of development of Malayalam dramas are delineated in Chapter 4. India had a dramatic tradition distinct from that of the West. Unlike the human struggle as depicted in the Greek tragedies, the creation of a feeling of bliss or *ananda* was the objective of *abhinya*, according to the Indian tradition. Drama had a mythological origin with God Brahma himself creating it. It was assigned a superior status by bestowing the status of the fifth Veda. In his book Natyasastra, Bharat Muni, the dramatic theoretician of India has provided elaborate account of various aspects of theatrical performance in minute detail. In that respect, he excels Aristotle, the dramatic theoretician of the West. Drama in India known as Sanskrit tradition, deteriorated in course of time. Nevertheless, some forms of performances of a rudimentary nature continued to prevail in various linguistic regions. Dramatic theatre on modern line was to appear only during nineteenth century at the behest of the British rulers.

Dramatic performances of primitive forms were in vogue in Keala even before the origin of Malayalam as a distinct language. Most of them were ritual performances enacted in temples. Foremost among them are *Kudiattom*, *Padayani* and *Teyyam*. Amog them *Kudiattom* is by far the oldest with continuous theatrical performance dating back to the ancient past. *Kathakali*, the world renowned dramatic genre of Kerala was evolved during the seventeenth century. However, even before the appearance of *Kathakali*, *Chavittunatakam*, a Christian dramatic genre was introduced in Kerala by the European missionaries. It took nearly two more centuries for the appearance of modern forms of drama in Kerala. It was the Tamil artists, who started the ball rolling by staging commercial drama in Kerala. Subsequently, Malayalee authors took up the mantle and started to stage drama. The advent of technologically mediated drama like the motion pictures and tele-serials began to appear during the twentieth century. As in other parts of the world, they pose serious threat to dramatic theatres in Kerala also.

After presenting various aspects and stages in the development of dramatic theatres, the study proceeds to examine the deeper implications of the threat from mediated drama to the dramatic theatres, by examining the cost and returns of dramatic theatres, the attitude of the actors towards drama in the context of competition from the technologically mediated drama and the behavioural pattern of the audience to different forms of drama.

In conformity to the the aforesaid lines, the study proceeds to uncover inter-alia the nature of the production units, the components of the cost of production and the volume of returns of theatrical drama by drawing evidences from Malayalam drama in Chapter 5. Being a joint product, stemming from the efforts of different factors or inputs, drama requires an organisational arrangement. In the jargon of economics, the organisational arrangement needed to produce a commodity is known as the firm. Dramatic theatres form the model of the firm in dramatic activity. Artists and other participants in the dramatic activities normally organise under the banner of a theatre with a master artist or director at the helm and stage the drama in front of an audience. As indicated earlier, Caves regards such a venture, as a contract between art and commerce. (see p. 81). The parties involved in the contract consist of the artists and non-artists whom he calls humdrum inputs. As he visualises, artists by themselves are not able to sell their products for which the service of the humdrum inputs is needed. The humdrum inputs by themselves are not in a position to turn out artistic products. Both the parties therefore enter into a mutually beneficial contract, work together and stage the drama in front of an audience.

Any cultural endeavour is a creative activity, which creates cultural values distinct from economic value. Normally works of art are devoid of commercial considerations. However, the artists who produce cultural value do not produce in the vacuum. Instead, economic considerations enter in the picture as an important constraint, since artist need money to live and other material inputs to create value. Based on such premises, Throsby has introduced, as indicated earlier, a threefold model of artistic organisation. (see p. 83). They are: (i) income constraint, (ii) income as a joint maximand, and (iii) income as the sole maximand. In the first instance, artists are content with the minimum remuneration to sustain themselves. Such a minimum is needed not as an incentive but as a minimum needed for creating cultural value. Most non-commercial theatres fall under this category. Such ideal conditions are rare in the actual world and artist may demand more income to secure better amenities of life. In order to uncover the new scenario, he introduces the second model, termed joint maximand. The objective function of this model can be stated as the joint maximisation of cultural and economic value, out of the works of art so that artists are entitled to secure better amenities of life. Most of the commercial theatres fall under this category. The third category, looks upon income as the sole consideration in producing works of art. Most of the cinemas and tele-serials and other components of the culture industry fall under this category, wherein income is the main consideration with art occupying an insignificant position.

According to the industrial sources, theatres fall under three categories viz; amateur, professional and experimental. The amateur theatres, stand very close to Throsby's first category which is by and large a non-profit organisation. The professional category consists mostly of commercial theatres which squarely cater the artistic qualities as well as commercial interests. The experimental category of theatre, is concerned with new forms of dramatic genres like the traditional forms and so on.

Since any drama is a joint work of different inputs, the cost of production would be fairly high. The main components of costs consist of those for script, cast, music, direction, training, rent, miscellaneous labour cost etc. Apparently, they are for artistic as well as for material inputs. Material inputs account for approximately one third of the total cost. However, there is no uniform standard in the proportion of any item of cost. Though actors provide the main input, the cost for their services is not very high as most of them engage in drama out of their keen interest in acting. Dramatic theatres or units, prepare a drama and stage it for a few days. Each performance remains as a separate activity and costs have to be incurred for each performance. In this respect, dramatic theatres differ very much from technologically mediated drama.

Being a service activity wherein the production and utilisation take place simultaneously, measurement of output becomes a baffling problem. If 'the service' is not utilised simultaneously with the production there will be no output at all. They are as Caves adds "experience goods" whose qualities cannot be assessed "before committing to consume them"[1]. Then, how to measure the output, let alone the value, poses as the problem. In order to surmount the problem, an indirect method is being adopted as a way out to measure the volume of output. It is by taking the volume of turn over as the quantum of output. With the appearance of the technologically mediated drama, turn over of dramatic theatres in the form of box office collections have declined considerably and most of the theatres fail to meet both ends. Invariably many of them subsist with the aid from public authorities and charitable organisations.

The impact of the technologically mediated drama on the career of artists forms the theme of the next Chapter. Literary writers, actors, directors, musicians and so on form the important category of artists who render different functions in any drama. It was the literary creators who had the upper hand in the past. At present, directors have emerged as an important class to whom the authorship of creativity is assigned by some scholars. In turn, directors are labelled as auteurs by some scholars. Their responsibility is to coordinate the functions of other inputs. However, it is the actors who, with their bodily gestures and histrionic talents, provide the most important inputs in any drama. Though most of the actors as a class are guided by creative impulses, money is required for their subsistence and accordingly, many of them have transformed themselves as providers of inputs in the material sense. However, productivity consideration in the determination of remuneration as in other activities cannot be applied in the case of artistic activities. Accordingly, wage rates of actors do not rise as in other occupations. At the same time, there has been wide variations in the actual volume of remuneration to different categories of artists. The entry of technologically mediated drama with the super stars at a commanding position has seriously compromised the position of dramatic actors. Inevitably, a situation in which most of the talented actors, seeking their fortune in television, where the rate is very high has emerged and consequently only the less talented stick on to drama. Actors, in Malayalam drama as a class get very low rate of remuneration. Most of them stick on to drama because of their inherent interest in acting. On the other hand, serial actors get very attractive rate of remuneration. Though many of them started their career in drama, they seem to be reluctant to go back to drama any more. Interestingly, students of School of Drama at Thrissur, whom we have interviewed seem to prefer a career in drama and very few among them entertain any desire to take up a career in television. Apparently, drama is able to survive because of the interest of some actors to remain thick and thin in drama.

Significance of the audiences in drama and their attitude towards different forms of drama form the theme of Chapter 7. In the normal sense, audiences constitute the third segment in a drama. Any drama is complete only when it is presented in front of an audience. They also acquire additional leverage, because it is, they who are supposed to recoup the cost of the performance by paying admission fee. A line of thinking to look upon audiences as mere consumers rather than as partners in a drama is on the anvil as an aftermath of the entry of technologically mediated drama. Though such a line of thinking may hold good in the case of technologically mediated drama, it can not be regarded as valid in the case of theatrical performance. Production of any commodity under capitalist conditions is meant for sale. On the other hand, production of arts and culture is not meant for sale like an ordinary commodity. They are creative activities through which the artist communicates the reality as he sees it. As a communication process, it is addressed neither to all, nor meant to satisfy anybody and everybody. In other words, the artists write to satisfy the interest of those who can understand and appreciate what he writes. Furthermore, the term appreciation rather than satisfaction is invariably adopted for expressing the benefits accruing by gazing the works of art. Under such circumstances, the rationale to club the audience as mere consumer cannot be treated as sound proposition.

In this context, the distinction of the audience as passive and active, can shed further light in the matter. Active audiences are supposed to be those who are able to decode the structural formations of drama and are capable of making meanings. On the other hand, passive audiences are those who are not in a position to create meanings of their own, except to accept meekly the intended meaning provided by the playwright. Audiences of drama have to be regarded as active participants who can draw their own conclusions and derive pleasure by seeing the drama. Instead, audiences of mediated drama behave like mere consumers of any commodity who "take a passive attitude to consumption, relying on the seller to supply the know-how and relieve him of the bother"[2]. Thus while the behaviour of most of the audiences of mediated drama resembles to that of mere consumers, the audience of theatrical drama retains the characteristics of active participants. In other words, while audiences of theatrical drama remain steadfast as audience proper who are capable of appreciating the dramatic performance, audiences of technologically mediated drama transform themselves as consumers of a commodity, like that of any regular consumers.

The functions and role of audiences in the context of such formulations are uncovered through a field study among the audiences of Malayalam drama. The audiences covered in the survey consisted mostly of the aged people. Youngsters were relatively few among the respondents. Most of the audiences are people who have seen at least one drama during the last one year. They are drawn from different strata of the society. Most of them are better educated. As things stand, the audiences are not in a position to provide enough financial support to drama as the size of the audience is shrinking. Only those who are committed to drama alone see the performances in a theatre. Though, they form only a minority, they seem to appreciate and enjoy dramatic performances in the theatre. On the other hand, technologically mediated drama manages to attract most of the audiences. Interestingly some of the hardcore audience of theatrical drama also see tele-serials apparently on account of their easy accessibility. The size of the audience of the technologically mediated drama has increased with further improvement in the living condition of the people.

The last Chapter deals with the policy options to be adopted for the survival of drama. Being the most ancient form of art depicting a true representation of life, drama deserves protection and support.

Furthermore, they give scope for local talents and a training ground for aspiring artists. However, with the fall in the size of audience, most of the theatres fail to recoup the cost of performance. Public support is the only option for the survival of drama in the face of stiff competition from the technologically mediated drama. New policy guidelines, like the grant of aid through the local bodies have to be thought of as a better option. At the same time, the need of the hour, is for incorporating traditional formats and adopting experimental genres as a viable alternative for meeting the challenge effectively. As Encyclopaedia Britannica enjoins "elite interest in folk forms generated new audiences in such forms and helped save traditions around the world that might otherwise have succumbed to industrialisation and cultural globalisation"[3].

Being an art, drama can be regarded as a communication medium addressed to an audience. Most of the arts manage to retain their legacy by addressing to an audience of their choice. Poetry is one among them, which is alive and kicking, though the size of the audience is shrinking. Similarly, what drama does is to communicate to an audience of its choice and not to any body and every body. Drama can survive on the same lines as poetry does by catering to the needs of a minority audience. Not surprisingly, Heilburn and Gray make the following observation on the hold of dramatic theatres on audience. They state: "And as in the case of dance, a work written thirty–or 130-years ago may still be new to the audience in a given town. So the theater certainly has the advantage of artistic novelty to build and hold its audience"[4]. No wonder, the caption, "Theatre audiences in Europe flock to plays despite the economic squeeze" of Guardian corroborates this aspect[5]. Moreover, being a public good, it has a legitimate right for support especially in the context of stiff competition from the technologically mediated drama. It also serves a medium suitable for giving expression to local talents and at the same time a training ground for aspiring artists. Not surprisingly, the following observation of Harvard Magazine stands as a reassuring assessment on the question of the survival of dramatic theatres. It observes, "experience cannot be replaced by anything viewed on the screen, in 3-D or interactively. The theatre will surely stay alive in the future—the only question is- in what forms?The hunger for live story-telling, for the shared experience of actor and audience, may even increase, if and when people tire of the edited, buffed, packaged perfection of television and film products"[6]. At the same time, the position of dramatic theatres resembles to that of the competition and coexistence of different species within the natural environment as visualised by niche theorists[7].

NOTES AND REFERENCES

1. Caves Richard (2000); *Contract Between Art and Commerce* (Harvard University Press) p. 179.
2. Scitovsky. T. (1972); "What's Wrong with the Arts is What is Wrong with Society" In Blaug Mark (ed.); *The Economics of the Arts* (London, Martin Robertson & Company) p. 61.
3. *Encyclopaedia Britannica (2014*); *Theatre Art: The Influence of Writing and Scholarship.*
4. Heilburn James and Charles M. Gray (2001); *The Economics of Art and Culture* (Cambridge, University Press) p. 39.
5. Guardian dated 27th July 2012.
6. http://harvardmagazine.com/2012/01/the future of theatre. p. 7.
7. Canclini. Nestor Gracia (2010); "Theatre and Performance in the Age of Global Communication" in Williams Gary Jay (2010); *Theatre Histories: An Introduction* (Routledge, Taylor and Francis Group) p. 464.

Bibliography

Abercrombie Nicholas (1996); *Television and Society* (Cambridge, Polity Press).

Adorno, T.W. and Max, Horkheimer [1972]; "The Culture Industry; Enlightenment as Mass Deception" in Curran James [ed.]; *Mass Communication and Society* (London, Open University).

Bakker Gerben (2008); *The Economic History of the International Film Industry.* (http//eh.net/encyclopaedia/theeconomichistoryof-international-film.industry/)

Bajaj Yogita and Mehta Sangita (2010); "Emerging Trends in Indian English Drama" in *Journal of Science and Commerce* Vol. 1 No. 1.

Blaug Mark (1976); *The Economics of Art* (17 Quick Street, London, Martin Robertson & Co).

Barker Chris (2000); *Cultural Studies: Theory and Practice* (New Delhi, Sage Publications).

Bhat. S.C. (1994); *Satellite Invasion of India* (New Delhi, Gyan Publishers).

Bhatia, Nandi (2006); *Modern Indian Theatre: A Reader* (New Delhi, Oxford University Press).

Blankstein Jane *et al.* (1987); *TV Careers Behind the Screen* (New York, John Wiley & Sons Inc).

Brandt George W. (1991); *Modern Theories of Drama* (Oxford University Press).

Brewswater Ben (1997); *Theatre to Cinema* (Oxford University Press).

Boulding, Kenneth (1973); "Towards the Development of Cultural Economics" in Louis Sneider (ed.); *The Idea of Culture in Social Sciences* (Cambridge University Press).

Bundy Penny; "Aesthetic Engagement in Drama Process" in *Research in Drama Education* Vol. 8. No. 2.

Burger, Anna (1970); *Economic Problems of Consumer Services*, (Budapest, Academia Kiado).

Burton Graeme (2010); *Media and Society: Cultural Perspectives* (New York, Tata Mcgraw Hill).

Butcher S.H. (2000); *A Translation of the Poetics of Aristotle* (The Pennsylvania State University an Electronic Classics Series Publication).

Canclini Nestor Gracia (2010); "Theatre and Performance in the Age of Global Communication" in William Gary Jay (ed.); *Theatre History: An Introduction* (London, Routledge, Taylor Francis).

Carlson, Marvin (1996); *Performance: A Critical Introduction*, (London. Routledge).

Caves. R. (2000); *Creative Industries: Contract between Art and Commerce* (Cambridge, Harvard University Press).

Collins Alan and Hand Chris (1998); "Making a Crisis out of a Drama: Should We Continue Public Financial Support for British Theatre?" in *Economic Issues*. Vol. 3, Part 2 September 1993.

Collin Jane and Andrew Nibset (2010); *Theatre and Performance: A Reader in Scenography* (London, Routledge Taylor & Francis Group).

Cheney Sheldon (1952); *The Theatre*; *Three Thousand Years; Drama Acting* and *Stage Craft* (Longman Green & Co. Inc).

Choondal Chummar (1984); *Christian Theatre in India* (Trichur, St. Thomas I.S. Press).

Curran James (ed.) (1991); M*edia and Society* (London and New York, Hodder & Stoughton).

Denise. D. and Bielby. P. William (2004); "Audience Aesthetics and Popular Culture" in Friedland Roger (ed.); *Matters of Culture*: *Cultural Sociology* (Cambridge Unniversity Press).

Dharwadker Aparna Bhargava (2005); *Theatre of Independnce: Drama, Theory and Urban Performance in India* (New Delhi, Oxford University Press).

Encyclopaedia Britainnica (2014); *Theatre* (*art*) *Drama; Search for Audience*.

Esslin Martin (1987); *The Field of Drama: How the Signs of Drama Create Meaning in Stage and Screen* (New York, Metheun).

Farley P. Richmond *et al.* (1993); *Indian Theatre Traditions of Response* (New Delhi, Motilal Banaridass Publications).

Fischer Ernst (1959); *The Necessity of Art: A Marxist Approach* (Penguin Books).

Fiske John (1987); *Television Culture: Popular Pleasures and Politics*. (Metheun & Co. Ltd.).

Fort B. Aloce Kates S. Herbert (1935); *Drama of the Middle Ages in Minute History of Drama* (*New York, Grosset & Dunlop*).

Gans Herbert. J. (1974); *Popular Culture and High Culture: An Analysis an Evaluation of Taste* (New York, Basic Books).

Hamilton Clayton (2004); *The Theory of Theatre and other Principles of Dramatic Criticism*; (Project Gutenberg, e-book).

Hancock Alan (1968); *Mass Communication* (London, Longman Green Co.).

Heilburn James (ed.) (2001); *Economics of Art and Culture* (Cambridge, The University Press).

Hesmondalgh David (2002); *The Cultural Industries* (London, Sage Publications).

http://harvardmagazine.com/2012/01/the–future of theater

Jain Nemichandra (1992); *Indian Theatre: Tradition, Continuity and Change* (New Delhi, Vikas Publishing House Pvt. Ltd).

Johnson Lousie C. (2009); *Cultural Capitals Revaluating the Arts: Remaking Urban Spaces*; (Surrey, Ashgate Publishing Ltd).

Joseph. K.V. (2010); *Economics of Culture Industry: Television in India*; (Delhi, Shipra Publications).

Joyce, Carey (1958); *Art and Reality* (Cambridge, University Press).

Jowett Garth and James. M. Linton (1980); *Movies as Mass Communication* (London, Sage Publications).

Kastaur Jayant (ed.) (2007); *Indian Drama in Retrospect*. (New Delhi, Sangeet Natak Akademi).

Kellener Douglas (1995); *Media Culture* (London, Routledge).

Kuspit Donald (2014); "Paradoxes and Problems of the Reproduction and Commodification of Art in the Age of Capitalist Spectacle" in http://www.per contra.net/arcive/19kuspit.htm

Lal Anand (2009); *Thetres in India: A Consise Companion*; (New Delhi, Oxford University Press).

Leach Jim (2004); *British Film* (Cambridge University Press).

Macgowan Kenneth and Melnitz, William (1955); *The Living Stage: A History of World Theatre* (Englewoods Cliffs, Prenticehall).

McPhail Thomas L. (2004); *Global Communication: Theories, Stakeholders and Trends* (Oxford, Blackwell, Publishers inc).

Manley Brian (2011); *Moving Pictures: The History of Earley Cinema* (Pro Quest Discovery Guides).

Mayer David and Richards Kenneth (1977); *Western Popular Theatre* (Metheun Young Books).

Merlin Bella (2010); *Acting: The Basics* (London, Routledge).

Mitra Anand (1993); *Television and Popular Culture in India*; (Delhi, Sage Publications).

Mullan Bob (1997); *Consuming Television: Television and Its Audience* (Oxford, Blackwell Publishers).

Munshi Shouma (2010); *Prime Time Soap Operas on Indian Television* (New Delhi, Routledge, Taylor and Francis Group).

Newman Z. Michael and Levine Elena (2012); *Legitimating Television* (Routledge, New York and London).

Oommen. M.A. and Joseph. K.V. (1991); *Economics of Indian Cinema* (New Delhi, Oxford and IBH).

Osborne Harold (1968); *Aesthetics and Art Theory: An Historical Introduction*, (London, Longman Green & Co).

Pick, John (1986); *Managing the Art: The British Experience* (London, Rihinegold, Publishing Company).

Pillai Sankara G. (1970); *Malayala Nataka Sahithya Charithram (Mal) History of Malayalam Dramatic Literature*) (Thrissur, Kerala Sahithya Academy).

Pillai Vayala Vasudevan (2005); *Malayala Nataka Sahithya Charithram* (Mal) *History of Malayalam Dramatic Literature* (*Thrissur*, Kerala Sahithya Academy).

Prakash Anand (2013); *Critical Interpretation of Englih Drama* (New Delhi, Wisdom Press).

Raphy Sabeena (1964); *Chavittu Natakam (Mal)* (Kottayam, National Book Stall).

Redmond James (ed.) (1979); *Drama and Society* (Cambridge, University Press).

Richmond Farley. P. (ed.) (1993); *Indian Theatres: Tradition and Performance* (Delhi, Motilal Banaridas Publishers Pvt. Ltd.).

Santana Ivani (2006); "Ambiguous Zones: The interwining of dance and world in the technological era" in *International Journal of Performing Arts and Digital Media* Vol. 2; No. 2.

Sayre Shay (2008); *Entertainment Marketing and Communication: Selling Branched Performances, People and Places* (New Delhi, Pearson Education Inc).

Schechner Richard (2003); *Performance Theory* (London, Routledge).

Sheehan Helena (2001); *Television as A Medium of Drama* (Dublin Rte, Dcu Course Social History and TV Drama).

Shervin Rosen (1981); "The Economics of Superstars" in *The American Economic Review* Vol. 71 No. 5.

Stam Robert (2000); *Film Theory: An Introduction* (Blackwell Publishers Inc).

Stanislavsky on the Art of the Stage translated by David Magarhack (London, Faber and Faber).

Steinert Heinz (1998); *Culture Industry* (Translated by Sally Ann Spencer, Cambridge Polity Press).

Shank Theodore (1994); *Contemporary British Theatre* (Palgrave Macmillan).

Sreekumar (2005); *Orumukham; Janpriyanatakavediyudmidipukal* (*Mal*) (Kozhikode, Poorna Publications).

Sreekumar. K. (2002); *Malayala Sangeetha Nataka Charithram* (Kozhikode, Poorna Publications).

Tallur Basavaraj. S. (2010); *The Western Drama.* (Atlantic Publishers and Distributors (P) Ltd).

Thornham Sue and Purvis Tony (2005); *Television Drama Theories and Identities* (Palgrave Macmillan Inc).

Tillis Steve (2012); "The Case Against World Theatre History" *in NewTheatre Quarterly*, Vol. XXVII, Part 4.

Towse Ruth (2010); *Cultural Economics* (Cambridge University Press).

Towse Ruth (ed.) (1997); *Boumol's Cost Disease: The Arts and Other Victims* (Cheltenham, UK Edward Elgar).

Throsby David (2001); *Economics and Culture* (Cambridge University Press).

Throsby David (2010); *Economics of Cultural Policy* (Cambridge, University Press).

Turner Graeme (2006); *Film as Social Practice* (Routledge, London and New York).

Val Jaine del (2006); "Situated Tekhne; Beyond the Performative: Metaformative Bodies and the Politics of Technology in Post-Post—Modernism" in *International Journal of Performance Arts and Digital Media*, Vol. 2, No. 2.

Vogel Harold. L. (2004); *Entertainment Industry Economics: A Guide to Financial Analysis* (Cambridge, University Press.).

Ward Ken (1989); *Mass Communication and The Modern World* (London MacMillan Education).

Williams Gary Jay (ed.) (2010); *Theatre Histories—An Introduction* (London, Routledge, Taylor & Francis Group).

Williams Raymond (1675); *Television, Technology and Cultural Form*; (London, Routledge).

Walter Benjamin (1997); "Work of Art in the Age of Mehaical Reproductuion" in Curran. J. (ed.) *Mass Communication and Society*. (London, Open University)

Zarrilli Philip. B. (2002); *Acting Reconsidered: A Theoretical and Practical Guide* (London, Routledge).

Index